Basil Hume

Basil Hume

Ten Years On

Edited by WILLIAM CHARLES

burns & oates

Published by Burns & Oates, a Continuum imprint

The Tower Building	80 Maiden Lane
11 York Road	Suite 704
London	New York
SE1 7NX	NY 10038

www.continuumbooks.com

First published 2009

Reprinted 2009

British Library Cataloguing-in-Publication Data
A catalogue record for this book is available from the British Library.

ISBN 9780826439413

The moral right of the editor and contributors to this volume has been asserted.

The Editor and Publishers are grateful to the following for permission to quote from copyright material:
Ampleforth Abbey for the chapter by Abbot Hume
Bishop John Crowley for his homily at Cardinal Hume's funeral.
Harper Collins for extract from Cardinal Martini's chapter in *Basil Hume by His Friends* (ed Carolyn Butler, copyright 1986) and extract from *Basil Hume: A Portrait* by Tony Castle and John Harriott and copyright 1986.
Hodder and Stoughton and Paraclete Press USA for material from *Searching for God*.
Hewan Dewar for extract from *History of Cardiology in Newcastle*.
Darton Longman and Todd and Paraclete Press USA for extracts from *Basil in Blunderland* by Cardinal Hume, copyright 1997.
Darton, Longman and Todd and Fortress Press for the poem from *A Thousand Reasons for Living* by Helder Camara and copyright 1981.
Farrar, Straus and Giroux for extract from *God in Search of Man* by Abraham Joshua Heschel and copyright 1955. Copyright renewed in 1983 by Sylvia Heschel.
Veritas Publishers for extract from *Pilgrimage of Grace* by Kevin Kelly.
Liam Kelly on behalf of The Estate of Cardinal Hume for extracts from various unpublished material.

* * *

Acknowledgement is also made to Ampleforth Abbey for permission to reproduce the portraits of Abbot Byrne and Abbot Hume and to Carlos Reyes-Manzo for permission to reproduce the photograph of Cardinal Hume in Ethiopia.

Typeset by BookEns Ltd., Royston, Herts.
Printed and bound by Antony Rowe, Chippenham, Wiltshire.

Contents

Contents

Contents

Foreword

The reader is entitled to know what sort of book this is. It is perhaps best to see it as a family memoir of my uncle, a tribute to a much loved member of the family ten years after he died. Because he was famous and important, it seemed to make sense to ask others to assist by supplying their own contributions to fill out the picture in a way that mere family memories could never achieve, in the hope that as a result the book would appeal to a wide audience. I am very grateful to all who have contributed to the book, which they have done without expectation of any financial reward. For them as for me it has been truly a labour of love.

This book is not a biography. The reader in search of that is directed to Antony Howard's beautifully written *Basil Hume, the Monk Cardinal* (Headline 2005). Nor does this book seek to provide profound scholarly insights into the spirituality of the subject we cover. Such an endeavour would be beyond my abilities. One day, I hope, someone might be inspired to produce a work which would aim to shed light on these matters. There are some comments on religion, but these are designed only to give the reader some suggestions of the most obvious influences which formed the man. There is undoubtedly much more which could be said to give a full account of the relevant issues.

This book should perhaps best be seen as a set of memories and reflections, providing a series of portraits, at different stages of his life, of a man who was both a monk and a cardinal, from a variety of people who knew him personally. If it is not presumptuous to say it, it is hoped that it may in some small way serve the Gospel message of love to which he devoted his life. He would have seen little purpose to the exercise if it did not.

Fuller acknowledgements are to be found at the back of the book. Principal among them are of course acknowledgements to those who have written chapters. I am deeply grateful to them. Their labours have made possible a publication which would otherwise simply not exist. I shall be forever in their debt.

In the text, some quotes, which come from published works, are referenced, but many are from private papers or personal interviews and are therefore not referenced. A number of chapters from the book result from a pooling of memories from a wide range of different sources. These have been collated by a number of people. In these circumstances, it is not appropriate to name individual authors, though the chapters have been subject to the same editorial processes as the rest of the book.

Sadly, I know from experience that nothing in which I am involved is ever without flaw. If the reader detects such flaws, I take responsibility and make apology.

William Charles

With great sadness I have received the news of the death of Cardinal George Basil Hume.

I offer prayerful condolences to the Auxiliary Bishops, priests, religious and laity of the Archdiocese of Westminster and to the entire Church in England and Wales.

Commending the Cardinal's noble soul to our heavenly Father's eternal love, I thank the Lord for having given the Church a shepherd of great spiritual and moral character, of sensitive and unflinching ecumenical commitment and firm leadership in helping people of all beliefs to face the challenges of the last part of this difficult century.

I am confident that the example of the Cardinal's devoted service as Benedictine monk and Abbot at Ampleforth and as Archbishop of Westminster, his untiring work as President of the Bishops' Conference, as well as his witness of dignity and hope in the face of the mystery of suffering and death will inspire all who knew him to ever greater fidelity to the Gospel of salvation.

Invoking the comforting gifts of the Holy Spirit upon the Cardinal's family and upon all who mourn him in the hope of resurrection, I cordially impart my Apostolic Blessing as a pledge of peace in Our Lord Jesus Christ.

Pope John Paul II
18 June 1999

Introduction

When Cardinal Hume died in June 1999, the response was remarkable.

The Queen sent a very moving message:

> I am so sad to hear of the death of Cardinal Hume. He will be remembered not only for his outstanding contribution to the Christian life of his country over recent years but also for the warmth, humour, and above all humility, which was such an example to us all. He will be much missed.*

The then prime minister, Mr Tony Blair, said, 'He was goodness personified, a true holy man with extraordinary humility and an unswerving dedication. He did much to inspire people of all faiths, and none.'

Similar sentiments were echoed by a variety of religious leaders. The Archbishop of Canterbury observed that for 'many ordinary people ... it was his personal qualities, especially his humility and compassion that gave him a special place in their hearts'. He spoke, too, of his own personal respect, admiration and affection. The President of the Methodist Conference said, 'We have lost an outstanding Christian leader.'

Chief Rabbi Sacks declared: 'Cardinal Hume is a tower-

---

*Private message sent from Her Majesty the Queen. 17th June 1999. Reproduced with permission from Buckingham Palace.

ing figure in the moral landscape of Britain and did more than anyone else to bring friendship and reconciliation between Catholics and Jews . . . [he] was a true friend to the Jewish people and we will cherish his memory.'

Iqbal Sacranie of the Muslim Council said, 'British Muslims sincerely grieve [his death] . . . all of us will miss his vision.'

This outpouring of affection and tributes to Cardinal Hume's holiness and love for his fellow man came from people of all walks of life. Both Catholics and non-Catholics spoke movingly of his kindness, his humility and his sense of humour.

The national press provided a snapshot of reactions from other people: 'He was our spiritual leader . . . a fantastic man and a great model to try to live up to'; 'I called him Your Grace, but he just said, "No, no, call me Father Basil" '; 'You didn't doubt God's existence when you were with Cardinal Hume. The Archbishop had clearly just been with him . . . He had the humility of a man who walked with God'; 'Cardinal Hume was a down-to-earth man. He brought all people together, Anglicans, Jews and Catholics. He bought *The Big Issue* from me. Sometimes he would say he didn't have any change and would buy it tomorrow – and he was always a man of his word.'

More than 10,000 people attended his lying in state. At his funeral there were 2,000 in the cathedral and another 2,000 were said to have crammed into the piazza outside – a reporter noted that their singing could be heard from Victoria station.

Why did this man cause people who had perhaps only met him on a single occasion – or never – to feel such love and admiration? The chapters which follow will try to explain.

PART ONE

The Making of an Archbishop

1

Formed in the Family

William Charles

The family is the first school of life and love. Each of us is marked indelibly by our own family and childhood experience.
Cardinal Basil Hume, *The Mystery of the Incarnation*,
(Darton, Longman and Todd, 1999)

My Uncle George once said that the three people who had been the greatest influences in his life were his mother, Abbot Byrne and Pope Paul VI. Later chapters will explore the role of Abbot Byrne, my uncle's predecessor as Abbot of Ampleforth, and Pope Paul VI, who made him Archbishop of Westminster, but it was his mother, Marie Elisabeth Tisseyre, who was the first and crucial influence.

'Mimi', as she was known, was born and baptised in Paris in 1897, the elder of two daughters. Her father, Joseph, was a young officer in the French Army, the son of General Tisseyre. Her mother, Jeanne Boutemy, was the daughter of a rich industrialist who owned a linen factory near Lille.

If this suggests a privileged upbringing, it would be only partly true. As a child of the military, my grandmother moved whenever her father was sent to a new posting. As a result her sister was born in Toulouse (and baptised

5

Germaine after the local saint). When her father was sent overseas, the family went with him and therefore my grandmother spent part of her early life in Peru, Tunisia, Morocco and Spain. This was not quite the stuff of exotic travels that it may appear and Mimi found it very unsettling, vowing that if she had children they would be given a stable upbringing.

Her parents were devout Catholics and naturally she too was brought up as a Catholic. She had an extraordinarily strong faith: she had no doubts that God existed and that he had sent his son Jesus Christ to redeem us, and that we would live on after death. Whether we would end up happy for ever in heaven or suffering eternally in hell was less certain.

Childhood letters show her perhaps a little more concerned with religion than would now be likely. Aged 13, she wrote to her lifelong best friend, Marie-Thérèse, apologizing for her failure to write sooner: 'Madame Gaussin tells us that the best way to be pardoned by God after a sin is to make an act of perfect love.' But, for the most part, her letters to her friend are full of normal girlish chat. When she had been in Peru for a few months, having been taken from the Dominican convent school in Paris where their friendship had blossomed, she wrote to Marie-Thérèse sadly: 'I still do not have a Peruvian friend.'

In 1914, when she was 17, her life was severely disrupted by the First World War. Her father, coming over from North Africa with the family, was seriously wounded in the fighting. Her grandparents' house near Lille, probably the nearest to a permanent home that she had, was occupied by the Germans. They stole the machinery from the linen factory and the business was ruined. She never saw either of her grandparents again, as both died before the war ended.

This upbringing marked her. Although intelligent, her education suffered and she always felt herself at a disadvantage. It was therefore a great event for her when, in the early years of the First World War, she met my grandfather, William Hume. It was another great moment when, in early 1918, she wrote excitedly to Marie-Thérèse:

> As for what Germaine has told you, well yes, my old love, it is true, I am at the moment of the great decision. It is even taken, my great decision, and I plan to write to you an official letter ... Almost the whole family has been warned. Tante [Aunt] Jeanne and Elisabeth are very well disposed towards me, Bon Papa is not very happy. Uncle Louis Boutemy, although deploring that he is a protestant, says that he only wants my happiness.

William Hume and Mimi Tisseyre were married in December 1918.

William Hume was a doctor serving with the British Army in Northern France. He had trained as a heart specialist and was practising in Newcastle at the outbreak of the war. His father, George, was also a doctor and had practised in Newcastle. He had come from Berwickshire where his father, the son of a blacksmith, had moved from teaching to farming. William Hume, a charming, charismatic, talented man of great integrity, was nearly 18 years older than his wife. Despite the considerable differences between the two, the marriage was a happy one. She loved him dearly, and he loved to tease her, for she had very little sense of humour.

Perhaps my grandmother's lack of joy resulted from the instability of her early years. Desperately shy, always busy, strict but often generous, at times very prejudiced, she was a terrible worrier ('unbelievable' is the word her daughter Frances uses). Once she went to the local priest to say that she was worried because everything in her life was going so well. He told her to be patient. One form her worries took was a determination to arrive at stations well before the train left because she hated running for them. Once, as a result, she arrived at the station very early and told the porter she wanted the London train. 'You're just in time,' he said and ran off with her bags, she running after him. He dashed across the station and threw the bags into a train. She had to jump in after them as the train moved off, and quickly discovered that she had been so early she had caught a train one full hour before the one on which she had planned to travel. Her children would tease her that she would worry about what to worry about next. It is unlikely she saw the joke. Later in life her worries took different forms. She was now a bit world-weary. At a wedding she said that on the whole she preferred funerals because then a person's problems were at an end whereas when they got married they were only just beginning. She was utterly devoted to her husband and was devastated when he died in 1960.

While William was alive, however, she lived for him and the children once they were born. The pair settled happily in Newcastle and very soon the Hume family began to increase: Madeleine was born in 1919, Christine in 1921, George in 1923, Frances in 1924 and John in 1928. My grandfather's career flourished, but required extremely hard work, which meant he had very little time to spend with his children, though he did take George to watch football matches.

William Hume was a gifted man. A good sportsman in his youth, he was a very fine doctor, with a great ability to diagnose a patient's illness. He said he could generally tell what was wrong when the patient walked through the door. He built a reputation as the best heart doctor in the North of England and was in great demand as a result, charging his rich patients considerable fees but treating the poor for free. He was also a brilliant teacher. Appointed professor of medicine, his lectures became legendary for their clarity and entertainment value. He loved to say, 'I think it is time I told you a "gruey story",' such as the occasion when a man had a haemorrhage at home which his quick-witted wife tended by stuffing the kitchen cloth into the hole in his chest. William was at the forefront of developments in heart medicine in his period, one of the first heart specialists to use electrocardiograms. He also played a key role in setting up the British Cardiac Club, the forerunner of the present British Cardiac Society. In this, his social skills played a part. A contemporary of his once wrote, 'When Hume came into a room it always seemed to brighten up a bit,' for he was an entertaining man who enjoyed a joke.

Some of these jokes were played on his wife. One year he sent her birthday cards of large ladies in bathing costumes on the beach, with messages like 'From all your friends at the convent'. At Christmas he once put the head of the turkey in her Christmas stocking so it was the first thing she saw when she woke up (it was just as well my grandmother was not squeamish). When she was learning English, he would teach her slang words in the local Geordie dialect knowing that she would then use them – most inappropriately – when talking to educated ladies.

My grandfather inspired great loyalty among his staff. When my uncle was appointed Archbishop of Westminster in 1976, a nurse who had worked with my grandfather wrote to the effect: 'If you are half the man your father was, you will do.' When the Cardinal Hume Centre offered cards to raise funds, a former medical student of my grandfather's ordered some: 'In memory of Professor Hume, father of the Cardinal, and a real Prince among men.'

George was a much longed-for first son. Mimi's family set much store by boys and her parents had been very disappointed 'only' to have had two daughters. My grandmother therefore doted on her 'Georges' (pronounced the French way). She prayed he would become a priest. Sadly, she did not know how to show her affection calmly and fussed over him far too much whenever she could.

But he was one of five and my grandmother had other responsibilities organizing the staff and the house which meant she had little time to devote to her children. As was common in those days, my grandfather's consulting rooms were in the family home. My grandmother had to make sure that the house was clean and organized when the patients arrived. She had to do the daily shopping, make sure the cook and maids knew what was required, and ran to answer the phone – which was always ringing – to make appointments. She saw the children in the afternoon, at teatime, when she insisted they speak to her in French.

The woman, therefore, who featured most in George's early years was Nurse Lockwood, who had charge of the children for ten years from 1924. Claire Lockwood was a wonderful nanny who, with an under-nurse, was responsible for keeping the five children relatively happy in a confined space. They had to be quiet, because of the patients. But she was fair, loving, strict but very gentle, and managed the nursery superbly. This was no easy task, especially with the lively and noisy George around. Like all families, there were fights among the children. His sisters remembered frequent shouts of 'Goodness sake, George, shut up!'

George was not only influenced by the people around him but also by what he saw. Some experiences affected him profoundly. When, he was only 3 or 4, he saw a coffin being carried through the streets of Newcastle. This was when he learned of death. What he saw began a process of thought about life and death, in which he found he was unable to believe that death was the end. Equally important was a simple story about apples which he himself told many times in later years:

When I was very young I was told about a small boy who went into a larder and seeing a large pile of apples wanted to take one. He knew he shouldn't without asking, but everyone was out, and as there were so many apples nobody would know if there was one short. That story ate into my soul because it was pointed out to me that although nobody would know, one person would know and that was God. So for years after I thought of God as someone watching me all the time to see if I was getting it right, and catching me out if I got it wrong. It took me 40 years to recover from that story.

On other occasions he told this story, he added that he was told God would punish him for his action. It is clear that part of George's religious upbringing was a strict faith based on fear.

My grandmother had a very black and white, pessimistic view of the world and part of this was a view of God which was rather frightening. She once told me she would have belonged to a group called the Jansenists if she had been alive in their day. This was a reference to a religious tradition within the Catholic Church – Jansenism – which was austere and gloomy, though virtuous. It was described as a view that people must 'pray as if everything depended on God and act as if everything depended on ourselves'. In later life George described it as 'a spirituality based on fear; the idea of the love of God was not in their way of thinking'.

If my grandmother introduced George to a frightening idea of God when he was small, she did much to offset this in the long run when she went to look for schools for her children (a choice William left to her as it had long been established that the children would be brought up as Catholics). She had heard of Ampleforth College, the Yorkshire boarding school founded by the Benedictines, and visited it. She met Father Paul, the headmaster, and was so taken with him and the beautiful Ampleforth valley that she

11

decided immediately that this was the school she wanted her sons to attend. In her usual, worried way she put their names down much earlier than was normal, causing Father Paul some wry amusement at her caution.

The children were originally taught by a governess but she died when George was six. He was sent to day school in Newcastle shortly afterwards, where for the first time he was made to feel an outsider. As a Catholic in a Protestant school, Church rules in those days prevented him attending school prayers.

His religious education fell partly to Father Alfred Pike, a Dominican friar, who took responsibility for George's preparation for First Communion. But Father Pike did much else as well. Newcastle in the early 1930s was suffering a terrible economic downturn, with mass unemployment. The priest visited the poor to help them in their desperate condition. When making these trips, he sometimes took George with him. As a result George formed the idea that he, like Father Pike, should become a priest and seek to help the poor. He recalled later:

> One of my very vivid childhood memories was of my home town Newcastle, seeing children in the streets often without shoes or stockings and their mothers in church wearing their husbands' caps. I remember being taken at the age of 8 or 9, by a zealous and devoted priest, to a very poor area of Newcastle into a succession of houses where the average number of occupants to a room could be about 12. It was in the early thirties and the experience imprinted itself firmly in my mind. Even at that age I was forced to compare my own good fortune with those who had not been born into my situation and the question 'Why for me this situation and why for them the other?' lodged itself firmly in my mind.

In 1933, at the age of ten, George was sent away to boarding school at Ampleforth's preparatory school, Gilling

Castle, where he spent a year. This largely ended his days in the North East, for from now on he spent eight months of the year away from home in Yorkshire. Every summer was chiefly spent in France, visiting his mother's parents, where he would play with his French cousins. In the spring he spent time in the Lake District with his family. Only the Christmas holidays, therefore, were now wholly in Newcastle. But he always had fond memories of the place and continued to support Newcastle United football team for the rest of his life.

George was not happy at Gilling, missing the emotional support of home. He found it a tough environment. He was lucky, though, that a kindly monk, Father Antony Spiller, took an interest in him. Father Spiller was a very gentle, lovable, humorous man. He had an endearing habit when the holiday period came round. He would board a train at random and when he liked the look of the countryside he would get out and spend his holiday exploring the area. His friendship with George changed this, at least for one year, as he joined the family on their holiday in France.

My mother thought George was transformed by his first year away from home. She saw an introverted boy changed into a happy extrovert and gave the credit to Father Spiller, but it may be she only saw what George wanted her to see. George talked in later life of his unhappiness at Gilling and of each of us being two people, the inner person and the outer person. Perhaps at this early stage in his life he had learned an ability sometimes to hide his true feelings.

After two years in the Junior School, George joined the Senior School at Ampleforth in 1936 and stayed there for the next five years. These seem to have been generally very happy ones. Taking the entrance exam for the school that summer, he shared a dormitory with two other boys, Cecil Foll and 'Archie' Conrath, both of whom became lifelong friends. In the evening they entertained themselves, sliding the chamber-pots from under their beds along the wooden floor in an improvised game of bowls. At an English boys' boarding school in those days, it helped greatly to be good at sport, and Cecil, Archie and George all proved good at rugby football. They played in the same school teams. George became captain of the first team, a position which carries much status as well as creating a natural circle of friends. In later life the team would meet up once a year to renew their friendship.

George remembered, however, that he did not win a scholarship in the entrance exam. This may have disappointed his parents for they expected a lot from him, though they believed their son 'had to work' to get results. Even towards the end of his life George remembered this perceived 'failure' saying to a friend, 'You know, I have realized I am not as stupid as I thought I was.' He remembered hearing his mother say to someone else, 'If George knew as much about his studies as he does about football, he would do very well.' He said, 'I never forgot that. I knew a lot about football then because I was interested and loved it.'

George's memories of the school at Ampleforth in the 1930s were very positive. In its valley, 80 miles south of Newcastle, it had been run by the Benedictine monks of St Laurence for over 100 years. It was a generally happy, innocent place, greatly influenced by the monks who ran it and did most of the teaching.

The presiding influence was the headmaster, Father Paul Nevill, whose charming personality had persuaded Mimi to choose this school for her son. Father Paul was a very remarkable man. He was an outstanding headmaster, a man of great vision and abilities. He had seen the need to expand the school and was in the process of achieving a huge success, recruiting both pupils and fine teachers in numbers. A wonderful history teacher, he made his lessons come alive with his stories of Victorian politicians. Warm, generous, energetic, open and trusting, profoundly Christian, he left his mark on all he taught. He was, above all, a great monk, faithful to his prayers and in cultivating humility. He kept a record of his life under the heading 'Progress, of a Failure'. The old monks in the monastery infirmary were, he said, the people really responsible for the achievements at Ampleforth. It was their prayers which were the key. But ultimately he gave the credit to God.

Two other monks who influenced George were his housemaster Father Oswald Vanheems and Father Stephen Marwood. Father Oswald was a fine monk and something of a stickler for order. One evening, as a prank, George turned a book in the house library upside down so that the title was at the bottom. The next morning he checked: the book was back the right way up.

Father Stephen's influence was felt throughout the whole monastery and school because of his great and obvious holiness. He is remembered as 'truly a man of God', a great man of prayer, exquisitely sympathetic, who did everything with zest and perfection, 'the living embodiment of the Love of God'. George remembered him in later years as an outstanding, hard working monk:

> We remember with admiration ... Fr Stephen Marwood: so obviously a man of God, a man who had reached a very high level of prayer, and yet, among us, was one of the busiest and most devoted of the brethren. To this day people quote him as having had a profound influence. And he was representative I think ... of the finest type of monk which this house has produced ... so fully a human being, so eminently human and humane.

Stories from George's schooldays suggest that he had a lot of fun. On one occasion in a rugby match, a player from the visiting school's team came running down the pitch with the ball. An Ampleforth player tackled him but only managed to remove his shorts. The player, now half-naked, kept running towards the touchline and Archie Conrath, facing him, did not know whether he was still trying to play the game or get off the field to find cover. Archie tackled him all the same, throwing the player on to the ground in the middle of some ladies who were watching. George and the other boys found this very funny and teased Archie mercilessly.

As a boy George had a reputation for kindness and in his last year became involved in setting up a movement to deepen religious life in the school. This drew on ideas popular at the time and inspired by a Belgian priest, Father Cardijn, who saw the importance of providing for the religious needs of ordinary people and involving them in the work of the Church. Father Cardijn founded organizations called the Young Christian Workers and Young Christian Students.

In his last two years at the school, George became close friends with another boy, 'Clarence' Smith, who was a year younger but another good rugby player and also good at cricket. Both were potential captains. So George, who was not good at cricket, said, 'I will have to become captain of rugby and you will have to become captain of cricket.' And so it turned out. George was a very good captain. A tremendously determined, enthusiastic player, he would give much encouragement to the other players before the match, reminding them of their strengths and telling them they could do things he could not.

But deciding who should be captain was a triviality compared to another looming decision. In 1940 Britain was at war with Germany. Clarence and George had both thought they had a religious vocation but were only too well aware of the call to fight for their country.

George's sense of vocation had developed down the years

and it is possible to catch glimpses of where his thoughts were leading. On one occasion he was required to write an essay on the subject 'Happiness'. This set George thinking about happiness: 'What is happiness?' he asked. 'Are people generally happy? Why are we happy at one moment and not at another?'. The word became a starting point in his search for God.

A second experience was love. George was very discreet about this so it is unclear to what he referred when he mentioned it later. Although he was certainly attracted to girls, there is no family record of any great romance. But, as he said, 'I began to learn that in some way we are made for love and that all true human love ... has in it something of the infinite and eternal.'

Another glimpse can be seen in George's growing awareness of the beauty of the world and poetry. He had spent most of his teenage years in the beautiful valley of Ampleforth, with annual visits to the open seascape and skies of the north coast of France and the glories of the Lake District. It is perhaps not very surprising, therefore, that the poet who captured his interest was Wordsworth. However, it was a particular aspect of beauty and of Wordsworth's poetry which struck him. It is best expressed in a passage which he quoted in later years, saying 'in *Lines Composed a Few Miles Above Tintern Abbey* (13 July 1798), in which Wordsworth described in enthralling terms his realization that nature could disclose the presence of God:

> And I have felt
> A presence that disturbs me with the joy
> Of elevated thoughts; a sense sublime
> Of something far more deeply interfused,
> Whose dwelling is the light of setting suns,
> And the round ocean and the living air,
> And the blue sky, and in the mind of man:
> A motion and a spirit, that impels

> All thinking things, all objects of all thought,
> And rolls through all things.'

This quite transformed his attitude to all created beings. Following these experiences, 'the search for God was now on. God had begun to mean something'.

The first question, though, was, if George was going to respond to this increasing sense of God's calling, then how should he do so? He had at first been attracted to the intellectual Dominican friars to which Father Pike, the priest in Newcastle, belonged. But his time at Ampleforth had shown him the Benedictine way of life followed by the monks there and he had become increasingly drawn to them. His mother, who wanted him to become a priest, may have favoured the Dominicans, as she had an aunt who was a Dominican nun and had herself been at a Dominican convent school. Eventually, the Benedictine Father Antony Ainscough, who was the gamesmaster at Ampleforth, seems to have been the decisive influence, assuring George that the Benedictines would also give him the intellectual training he needed. The fact that Ampleforth was responsible for many parishes was also important, as he still wished to be a priest for ordinary people. In the autumn of 1940 George told another of his friends, Christopher Hatton, that he had decided to join the Benedictines rather than the Dominicans. (Christopher, or 'Stooge' as he was known in the school, himself joined the monastic community at Ampleforth in January 1941.)

The question still remained, however, whether he should join the monastery immediately or go into the armed forces first to fight in the war against Hitler. According to Clarence, in February 1941 the two of them went for a smoke (against the school rules) to discuss the situation. Clarence recalled that they concluded that the war was lost and that therefore they would better serve their country by joining the monastery and becoming priests. George seems to have thought that the Nazis might put monks in a concentration camp or execute them, so this was a brave decision. If this seems a little strange looking back, it is worth remembering that at this stage Britain was on its own against Germany which, with its allies, controlled most of mainland Europe, and clergy were being executed.

Clarence and George applied to join the monastery in March 1941 and were accepted as postulants for entry in September. As George left home in Newcastle to join the monastery, he called back jokingly, 'Pope or bust!' (mimicking the war slogan 'Berlin or bust!'). His sisters shouted back 'Bust!'

2

Formed in the Monastery: Ampleforth Recollections

For many people today the word 'Ampleforth' may have connotations of a school, Ampleforth College, often referred to as 'the Eton of the North'; or an abbey, 'the place where Basil Hume was abbot'. First and foremost, of course, it is a monastery, even today one of the largest Benedictine monastic communities in Europe. The monks continue to be involved in a number of works: two schools (Ampleforth College and St Martin's Ampleforth), St Benet's Hall (a Permanent Private Hall of the University of Oxford), a monastic foundation in Zimbabwe, and about a dozen parishes in the immediate environs of the abbey and further afield in the North West of England. Like many religious orders, the monks of Ample-forth are facing up to the challenges presented by an ageing community and yet still a large number of pastoral, educational and parochial commitments.

While statistics paint only a limited picture, co-educational Ampleforth College today boasts over 600 pupils, nearly 30 per cent of whom are girls. And the monastic community numbers just under 80 monks, 14 of whom work full-time in the college.

What a far cry from the school that Basil Hume left in the summer of 1941 and the monastic community he joined in September of the same year. He left a school of just over 350 boys and entered a monastery of over 130 monks, nearly 40 of whom worked full-time in Ampleforth College. Two years previously, in April 1939, the monks had elected as abbot Dom Herbert Byrne OSB, a man who would remain in charge of the community until the election of Basil Hume himself exactly 24 years later.

Ampleforth Abbey was home to a thriving, confident monastic community. Devotion to the duties of prayer and work were the hallmarks of Ampleforth monasticism. Behind these, too, was a keen sense of personal frugality and asceticism – the spiritual training and self-discipline required to focus on and devote oneself entirely to God's will. By and large monastic life was seen as an individual vocation characterized by prayer, obedience and hard work. For the novices entering the monastery in 1941 these would be the three key virtues that they would have to develop. One of the main things that united the monastic community was the sense of a 'shared' work in the schools – Ampleforth College and the preparatory school at Gilling Castle. Since so many of the monks had been or were still involved in teaching in the schools, and may well have been students there themselves, there was a common language, a common experience that provided a degree of unity within the community that bound them together. This positive aspect also had a flip side, however, for it meant that in training young monks less emphasis was placed on developing a sense of community identity. This would come through some process of osmosis, so the important thing for young monks was to develop their own sense of prayer, obedience and hard work.

Basil Hume had had what many might term a successful time in the school. Now, in September 1941, he and five other students from the college – Kentigern Devlin, Ian Petit, Luke Rigby, Julian Rochford and Brendan Smith – made the transition from classroom to cloister. After an eight-day retreat they were clothed in the black habit of the Benedictine monks and received their 'new' names – it was from this moment that George 'became' Basil. As if all of this was not enough of a shock, 18-year-old Basil Hume found getting used to the long black Benedictine habit quite tricky. 'For the first week,' he said, 'one was always tripping over it, especially going upstairs. It seemed to be a symbol, or parable, of what life as a religious is like – often tripping over.'

The monastic life is one in which the monk is seeking God above all things: 'Your way of acting should be different from the world's way; the love of Christ must come before all else', states the *Rule of St Benedict* (RSB 1980, 4.21), the book which was to become the guiding text for Brother Basil and his fellow novices.

When Basil himself became abbot, he often used to speak of four foundations of monastic life: prayer, obedience, humility and poverty. And from these four came charity, or love. In Benedictine monasteries it is the job of the novice master to teach the young novices about the monastic life. For the six new novices who had been clothed in September 1941 that task fell to Father David Ogilvie Forbes.

Perhaps one of the first things that would have struck these new arrivals may have been the silence. They would have been told, as they were taken up the stairs to their spartan cells, that there was to be no talking above the cloister. The first lesson was silence and observance.

Basil and the other novices were then in effect 'on trial' with a great emphasis on obedience and keeping the rules. In one sense, then, the novitiate was thought of as simply one step higher than sixth form, from where the young novices had come. There, they had been at the top of the ladder; now they were the ones being watched by the rest of the monastic community.

The discipline of the monastic life was something that was undoubtedly drummed into the novices. Basil seems, perhaps a little surprisingly, not to have been well prepared for this. One of the first things that he and Brother Brendan were told to do by the novice master was to go and scrub the floor of one of the rooms in the monastery. When they started work, Basil said somewhat disconsolately, 'I was not expecting this.' The following morning the novice master sent them to go and scrub the same floor again. They had, in their innocence, walked on the wet floor, and had left marks behind them. Novices were kept in their place. If a novice broke something, or made a mistake, he would have to go to the novice master to beg pardon and penance. This was not mere formality: if, for example, a novice had forgotten to take a breakfast or supper tray to the sick brethren in the infirmary, then that novice would have to kneel in the refectory holding out a tray until the abbot signalled the end of the penance.

To the modern reader, such disciplines will almost certainly seem extreme. But the aim was to help the novices focus every aspect of their lives on dedicating themselves to God. The *Rule of St Benedict* begins thus:

> Listen carefully, my son, to the master's instructions, and attend to them with the ear of your heart. This is advice from a father who loves you; welcome it, and faithfully put it into practice. The labour of obedience will bring you back to him from whom you had drifted through the sloth of disobedience. This message of mine is for you, then, if you are ready to give up your own will, once and for all, and armed with the strong and noble weapons of obedience to do battle for the true King, Christ the Lord.
>
> (RSB 1980, Prologue, 1.3)

Basil remembered reading the *Rule of St Benedict* for the first time and finding, somewhat to his discomfort, a statement which made it clear that hardships and trials are means of journeying towards God. From his bare monastic cell, with its bare, unsealed floorboards, iron bedstead and little furniture, the hardships must have appeared all too real. The wartime monastery was cold, dark, dusty and gloomy and there was no hot water early in the morning. Some of the novices used to get a jug of hot water at night, wrap around it their manual labour clothes and in the morning the water would still be warm enough for shaving. It seems that at the outset Basil was very depressed, and in fact went to the novice master to say, 'I feel as though I've come to die.' 'You have,' came the reply. The religious life was not going to be easy.

A novice's day was certainly full. From rising at 5 a.m. until as late as 10 p.m. every moment was accounted for – and the novice master made his charges complete a diary, filling in every quarter of an hour everything they did from getting up until they went to bed. Novices, as well as boys from the school, were expected to act as servers for the monks at Mass, especially outside term time. In those days, each monk celebrated his own Mass each day (hence the large number of side-altars in many churches).

One of the main focuses of study for the novices was, of course, the *Rule of St Benedict*. Other topics included scripture, plainchant, Church history and the rules of monastic living. There was a weekly conference from the novice master, as well as the weekly chapter, which the abbot gave to the whole of the community. The novices were encouraged to do their own spiritual reading and weekly confession was also encouraged.

It was largely through these weekly conferences and chapters and their own spiritual reading that the novices, and the monks, learned about monastic spirituality and prayer. Prayer was, and still is, central to monastic life, with the day structured around the times of the various 'offices' in the abbey church, the singing of the psalms in choir. At the start, Basil did not take to the psalms. He recalled later:

> We prayed the psalms ... I remember how hard I found it then to pray in Latin ... and the time spent in prayer often seemed long, and, I must admit rather tedious. It took me quite some time to realize an important truth: I wasn't there in the choir stalls of the abbey church to enjoy myself, I was there to worship, praise and give thanks to God. I was there for him and not for myself. Then I began to notice how I really did want to be at prayer with the other monks and slowly I began to understand the psalms, how rich they were and how they seemed to express all the needs and aspirations of a world always in turmoil.

At the outset, however, Basil found that his prayer life was less satisfying than he had hoped. He was not alone in this. In later life he recalled that in the monastery:

> We used to talk of the first fervour of the novitiate – it's always terribly easy in the first week, then it began to get difficult! We used to have a second meditation in the evening; there were six of us and I was always terribly upset because I could see the angelic expressions on the faces of the other five and wondered what they had that I hadn't got! This went on for some weeks until we got to know each other well and all defences were down and we then discovered that we all thought the other five were getting on very well.

The reality, of course, was that, 'We all agreed that we were bored stiff!' For Basil, it would be some time before he found satisfaction in his prayer life. He later compared prayer to drinking beer – the first experience is not usually enjoyed, but if we persevere we develop a taste for it.

One of the novices who joined the monastic community a matter of months before Basil Hume said that it was 'A rigorous novitiate, physically black, too, because of the war and the blackouts. Silence ruled. The emphasis was on external formation to a way of life; internal formation was something between the individual and his confessor.'

Looming behind all of this, of course, was the ongoing war. Abbot Herbert Byrne had the unenviable task of maintaining the monastic life of his monks. Many people with Ampleforth connections – teachers, old boys – had joined the forces and three monks served as military chaplains. New novices, including Basil Hume, were told, 'Your contribution to the war effort will be in your observance of the rules' (interestingly, the Basil Hume intake was the last major intake of novices until 1946, when ten joined the community). At a very practical level, every window had to be blacked out every night, a task which fell to the novices. However, the blacking out of windows – which, it seems Brother Basil often had to be reminded about ('I have a very bad memory. When I forget to put up the blinds in the evening, Father Abbot does it; and when I forget in the morning, Father Prior does it') – was perhaps not the most pressing thing on Basil's mind. In joining the monastery, he began to seriously question whether he had made the right decision: not only was his prayer life disappointing, but he was affected by scruples – an exaggerated concern about whether things have been done correctly or whether, in fact, they are sinful. If not tackled and resolved, this anxiety can lead to a severe scrupulosity resulting in a complete paralysis of action, a fear of doing something in case one might commit sin. Fortunately for Basil, worrying though the problem was, it never got so severe.

But if this was not bad enough, it seems that Basil, and indeed others in the novitiate, may also have begun to feel frauds in the monastery. Basil had joined the monastery thinking, perhaps, that defeat in the war was inevitable and so there was little point in joining the forces. But it was rapidly becoming clear that the war was not lost. Furthermore, the monastic community would receive news of old boys killed or wounded in the war and all were affected by this, especially the young novices who had chosen to join the monastery rather than fight for their country. Basil Hume and others began to have crises of conscience.

He took his problems to Father Placid Dolan, a wise, much-revered monk who had joined the community at Ampleforth in 1896. He suffered crippling asthma but had responsibility for a garden in which the novices worked in the afternoon. He was also a confessor to the young monks. In his own gentle way, Father Placid painted a picture of a God who cares for his creation; that Christ is in a mysterious way alive in the souls of all who are baptized and that God loves the Christ he sees in every human. To the Basil who had been advised that the only way out of his problems was to try harder and obey, this was just the assurance he needed: that God loved him and he really should not worry so much about things. Whatever the overall effect on Basil, however, he eventually confided in Father Placid that he planned to leave the monastery. Father Placid was going away for health reasons and persuaded Basil to stay in the monastery until he got back. In December 1941 Father Placid left Ampleforth and never returned.

Three other figures were extremely influential in the novitiate of Basil Hume: Father Kenneth Brennan, Abbot Bede Turner and Abbot Herbert Byrne.

Father Kenneth Brennan was born in Ireland in 1906 and ordained a priest for the Archdiocese of Glasgow in 1930, but joined the Ampleforth community eight years later. Full of laughter, he was very good at counselling others on an informal basis. He was described as:

> a man intensely interested in people ... who saw pretty
> clearly into the reality of what life is ... He knew the
> limitations of men and women, their weaknesses, and he
> knew how to love, encourage and support them ... for
> companionship, counselling and friends he was sought after
> by all the generations.

He gave Basil much help and became his confessor and friend for 40 years.

Abbot Bede Turner had been procurator (bursar) at Ampleforth from 1902 to 1936, when serious illness meant that he had to relinquish administrative responsibilities. However, he remained active and well into his seventies he would teach the novices each day about the rubrics of monastic life. To novices constantly being told about the importance of obedience and hard work he conveyed something about the warmth of monastic life. Abbot Turner died suddenly in 1947 at the age of 79 and his obituary stated: 'To the whole community he was a ready source of knowledge and counsel and fun and an admired example of goodness'.

But perhaps the greatest influence of all was Abbot Byrne, the man whom Basil himself was to succeed as abbot in 1963. Abbot Byrne did not have much direct contact with the novices, although, if any wanted to see him, they could. But the abbot sets the tone of the monastery and it is clear that Herbert Byrne was a great abbot. Most importantly he was a great monk. Austere, frugal, unsparing of himself, he was a great man of prayer, had total integrity and was very holy.

Kevin Herbert Byrne was a native of Birkenhead and started school at Ampleforth College in 1895. He became a monk and after further studies elsewhere joined the staff of Ampleforth College in 1909. At that time, there were about 30 monks in the monastery and 130 boys in the school.

Father Herbert, as he was then, taught classics, mathematics and music, was responsible for the school timetable, and, after it was adopted in 1911, was involved in rugby football. Father Herbert also became subprior and junior master in the monastery and the workload eventually took its toll. In 1935, he was appointed assistant priest in St Peter's parish, Seel Street, Liverpool.

The parish apostolate seemed to offer him a new lease of life and Father Herbert's early impressions have a particular resonance even today:

> It is the Mass that matters, and a natural and necessary means of learning to understand the people is to watch them at Mass ... kneeling among them at the back of the church. It is a fruitful experience. One's first thought is likely to be a harsh one about the designer of the benches, who was surely either misshapen himself or singularly indifferent to the happiness of his fellow creatures. The number of man hours of discomfort attributable to him must be immense. But there are more difficult matters. In an average congregation 10 per cent use books, 20 have [rosary] beads in their hands; of the rest, the small people wriggle unhappily, the larger ones lean heavily on the bench-rail. Are they praying? It would be rash to say they are not, and yet the daily difficulty of mental prayer after years of practice suggests a doubt. Certainly most of them do not seem to be praying. What they seem, misleadingly or not, to show is vacancy, weariness and a great patience: vacancy, because their minds do not easily form thoughts, nor does the Mass stimulate a flow of thoughts in them; weariness, because having nothing to think about they also have nothing to do; patience, because, apart from other reasons, they are wonderful people.

One of the first things Father Herbert did when he became parish priest at Seel Street in 1938 was to replace the benches.

Father Herbert's pastoral time in Liverpool came to an end in April 1939 when he was elected Abbot of Ampleforth, a post he held for the next 24 years. Abbot Herbert 'brought a new humanity into the life of the community: ... His own total integrity and humility, and the general awareness of the burden he bore until nearly the end of his seventies, gave him a moral authority of an unusual kind', were the words of one obituary. For someone in trouble, Abbot Herbert could always write words of comfort:

> I have found in my life that things do nearly always come right; and that situations which seem hopeless, and hope-lessly complicated, straighten out and turn into much better conditions. They do. Time after time I have found it so; and nearly always in some unexpected manner or through some agency on which one had not counted. I suspect God wishes to show us that our prudence is tiny and inadequate. We have to use it; but He produces much better plans and solutions.

One of the most significant lessons Abbot Byrne gave his monks was in the importance of perseverance. He taught them, regarding the always difficult but essential matter of prayer, saying, 'Trying to pray is praying. You must go on and on and on and on.' His monastic ideal was ascetical rather than mystical, and he was sceptical of enthusiasm for contemplation: 'Anyone who thinks he is praying for more than two minutes and a half is deluding himself,' he would say; and on hearing of a book called *Difficulties in Mental Prayer* he remarked that it must be a very large book.

Abbot Byrne was a huge influence in the community. He gave excellent short weekly chapters to his monks about the monastic life. He always put monastic discipline and values first, a fact highlighted at the end of the Second World War when the community was looking forward to Basil and the other young monks returning from Oxford to teach in the

31

college. Abbot Byrne was determined that monastic training must come first and sent some of the monks, including Basil, to study theology in Fribourg, saying, 'I suppose one is *less* likely to get a knife in the back in Switzerland than in other places abroad,' and that Fribourg was, 'A place where there is no Communism'!

But his life was itself the best way of teaching. For an abbot teaches above all by example, showing by deeds rather than by words, by his reactions to events, how a Christian should live, loving God and his fellow humans. When Basil Hume was elected abbot in 1963, he inherited from Abbot Byrne a community of 157 monks. Basil always retained the highest regard for Abbot Byrne and kept a photograph of him for the rest of his life. He said: 'My predecessor was a very, very holy man.' In later life he remembered him as an example of an obedient monk and recalled him, when he was abbot, calling his monks to humility: 'Remember fathers, when you die, someone will be relieved!'

In mid-1942, Abbot Byrne appointed a new novice master, Father Laurence Buggins, who had already been prior of the community for seven years (an office he held until 1951). Prior Buggins knew the novices well and this down to earth Lancastrian brought a practical outlook to the management of the novices. He was no academic but was imbued with a spirit of discipline and monasticism. When a monk, suffering scruples, tried to go back to confession straight after finishing, he called out in a Lancashire accent, 'Eeee, get out, Father!' He also brought lighter moments to the novices' lives. One day, they were studying a psalm that had been badly translated into Latin and so asked Prior Buggins what it meant. The prior thought for a while and then said, 'Eeee, it is a mystery!' The novices took this up as a catchphrase, saying, whenever the opportunity arose, 'Eeee, it is a mystery!'

Basil and the other novices were still kept very busy.

There was manual labour each afternoon, which could be a chore, but, at the same time, was an important opportunity for getting rid of youthful energy! And some of the tasks would certainly do that: sweeping up leaves in the Monks' Wood, chopping up trees, weeding in Father Placid's garden, picking potatoes, and, of course, in the winter, shovelling snow. On Thursday afternoons the novices had time off. This meant going for a walk or a long-distance run, which was usually Basil's preferred option.

Basil did not discuss his spiritual problems with the other novices. To them, he seemed a fun figure, often at the centre of the tricks that novices would get up to. On one occasion he and another monk pretended to be prospective parents visiting to see if they should send their boy to the school. The pretence ended when Basil's false moustache came away. On another occasion, Brother Martin and he tried to bash out a nail that was sticking out of a boot by knocking it on a fire extinguisher. The inevitable happened: the contents of the extinguisher shot over the monastery corridors and out of a window. The two young monks had great difficulty sorting out the mess, and all of this while observing the rule of silence!

The first year of the novitiate was marked by what are known as 'perseverances'. Every three months the novice master would provide the Abbot's Council with a report on the young novices, and the Council would give permission for each novice to continue or advise him that his vocation might lie elsewhere. On the fourth perseverance, the decision was put not just to the Council but to the whole of the monastic community, so that each monk could give his opinion about the novices.

With permission to stay, Basil made his simple, or temporary vows in September 1942, at the end of his first year. A monk remains in simple vows for at least three years and this turned out to be a decisive moment in his life, for

Basil rightly perceived his vows very seriously as a personal commitment to God.

At the end of his simple vows Basil made his solemn profession as a monk. It was September 1945. The war was over and any temptation to leave the monastic life and join the forces no longer had any pull for him. He committed himself to Ampleforth for life. However, he did this only after having had what he called 'a conventional crisis' which he said one had to have, 'otherwise it wouldn't be a deliberate decision'.

Basil took his solemn vows on 23 September 1945. In a ceremony rich in symbolism he took vows of obedience to the abbot and community, of stability (to remain a monk of Ampleforth for life) and of conversion of life (to live according to the *Rule of St Benedict*). Before the altar he recited three times the words of Psalm 119: 'Accept me, O Lord, as you have promised, and I shall truly live; and let me not be confounded in my hope' – '*Suscipe me Domine secundum eloquium tuum et vivam; et non confundas me ab expectatione meam*' – a text that Basil copied into the back of his own Book of the Psalms and one which, according to the monastic tradition, would be sung three times by the monks of Ampleforth Abbey at his funeral in 1999.

Before the abbot and the community, Basil signed the document of profession and then at the end of the ceremony retired to his cell for a three-day retreat of total silence away from the rest of the community. Basil later told a young monk that the three days of his solemn vows were the happiest days of his life. He recalled:

> In my personal experience, I found that a most tremendous liberation – the day I took my final vows. I was now set on my course for the rest of my life. It is a most moving ceremony when you stand before the altar and commit yourself in that way to God.

Basil would say that people often join monasteries for the wrong reason and stay for the right one. He probably thought this applied to him, too. Again, in the back of his Book of Psalms he wrote many years later the Latin phrase '*bonum est quia humiliasti me*' – 'it is good that you have humbled me'. Perhaps this referred to his early years in the monastery when he found that he, like everyone else, was flawed and capable of making mistakes, but should look to the future with hope, faith and vision, expressing a firm desire to change, a willingness to grow and learn.

Just over 25 years later, Basil was to write that his generation:

> imagined itself to be called to the monastic life. One did it because one thought this was right and one responded. The question of whether it fulfilled us or not didn't really arise, because one just got on with it, and maybe because we sought fulfilment less consciously we found it more quickly. One took the knocks and got on with it – but essentially it was a response and I think one realized and accepted that life wasn't roses anyway and one didn't want it that way. If one was going to give oneself to this life, one realized that it meant a sacrifice.

These first years in the monastery clearly left their mark. A contemporary at school, John Ryan, had found Basil then to be simply another rugby 'hearty'. When he went back to Ampleforth a few years later he found him transformed into a 'spiritual man'.

Soon after his election as abbot, Basil Hume gave a chapter at the clothing of some novices. Who knows if his words were in fact reflections of his own novitiate:

> Life in the novitiate will be circumscribed and the things you will be given to do will be, in the eyes of men, small, unimportant, and frankly rather dull. That can be irksome.

But learn, learn in the first week, that everything you do and everything that happens to you must be seen as an opportunity to deepen your love of God; that everything you do and everything that happens to you is to be enjoyed, or suffered, whichever it may be, with and through Christ. You are seeking God in community and you will soon discover what joy it is to live in community; what support you get from sharing with others the same ideals, the same aspirations, the same way of life ... Ours is a great life, a great vocation, and in it you will find joy and peace: a peace which no man can take from you.

And he gave the novices two key phrases: 'confidence', which he said was 'a boundless trust in God's goodness'; and 'yearning love ... the love for God which is the point of the monastic life'.

Basil's final word to novices nearly 30 years after his own clothing as a monk of Ampleforth was: 'And finally, don't take yourselves too seriously. Take life seriously. Take God seriously. But don't, please don't take yourselves too seriously!'

3

Ordination

William Charles

Brother Basil studied history at St Benet's Hall, Oxford from 1944 to 1947. He then attended Fribourg University in Switzerland from 1947 to 1951, where he took a degree in theology.

In 1950 he was ordained a priest and so became Father Basil. The memories of this day stayed with him for the rest of his life. He remembered it always as a very precious day: 'many thoughts went through my mind on that day and one quite especially so. Whatever might happen in the future no one could deprive me of the priesthood.' He once asked some fellow priests: 'Don't you remember the sense of joy and pride on the thought of just being a priest? What if I lived to celebrate Mass once and no more? I remember asking myself. Yes that would have been enough.'

4

Basil Hume as Schoolmaster

Richard Thomas
Old Boy of St Bede's House

The art of schoolmastering can be summed up quite simply: it is to teach boys to teach themselves – to teach boys to teach themselves how to live, how to pray, how to work, how to direct their lives, how to shoulder responsibility and so forth.
Cardinal Basil Hume, *Searching for God*, 1977

Father Basil Hume was a housemaster at Ampleforth for eight years from September 1955. Before that he taught history and French in the school for several years, and coached the school First XV. It was as a housemaster and a rugby coach that he made the most impact. Most of the people who saw him in action during that time considered him a very good schoolmaster. 'Wonderful', 'amazing', 'exceptional', 'the best housemaster by a country mile' are the views of some of those who passed through his House.

When Father Basil took over as housemaster at St Bede's he arrived with certain advantages. He was seen by the boys as relatively young and was preceded by a reputation as a good-natured rugby coach, fun for young people to be around. Those in the know in his House were delighted that he was to become their housemaster. Other houses envied them their good fortune.

One old boy of the House recalls meeting him before he became housemaster and the sort of impression he could make:

> One morning in the winter of 1954/5, with the other first-year boys from Bede's, I was required to wait in the passage at the junction of the school and monastery for monks who came out of morning prayer and needed a server for their individual Masses ... This tall young monk came out of the church and lifted his hand, and, it being my turn next, I followed him to some small chapel in the heart of the monastery where he vested and said Mass, my serving him. At the end of the Mass it came to the time to say the 'Prayers for the conversion of Russia', and he knelt down with his arms on the altar of this small chapel, and his head on his arms, and proceeded to lead the prayers, I responding. But he stopped, and so I waited. It occurred to me that he had fallen asleep but I did not presume to stretch out and nudge him. He soon woke though, and looking round him, said something like, 'Gosh, I must have fallen asleep,' smiled sheepishly, and then asked, 'Where was I?' I told him and we resumed.
>
> I don't think he knew who I was then, but that evening I bumped into him coming out of ... class, while I too was transferring to my next class. He saw me and said, 'Hello, we met this morning, didn't we? I fell asleep, didn't I?', and he smiled at me. Needless to say I was won over completely – and remained so throughout his life.

The initial ideas about this jovial, enthusiastic house-master were confirmed by the lighthearted way he distributed the boys' mail at breakfast – flicking their letters across the dining hall over the boys' heads, sometimes into their porridge – and by the lively way he woke up the big dormitory in the morning by clapping out the beat of Clarke's 'Trumpet Voluntary'. He soon turned his study into a common room, where boys could read a variety of newspapers which he bought for them. He also bought a record player and a carefully chosen collection of classical music, including fine recordings of Beethoven and Verdi's *La Traviata* and *Il Trovatore*, which he played for their benefit, later adding some jazz. He let the boys listen to popular radio programmes and the sports news, asking them to tell him the Newcastle United score if he wasn't there. The House quickly acquired a special reputation, helped by success at sports against other houses.

This helped Father Basil in his first years as housemaster. The boys were inclined to respond positively. With time, this changed as each intake was more likely to take its good fortune for granted. Later still, the cultural climate changed. The 'swinging sixties' brought in a wave of permissiveness. The prevailing ethos became pleasure-seeking and materialistic. This proved a more challenging environment in which to teach the values in which Father Basil so strongly believed.

In the early years, however, the climate was very propitious. In tackling the job, Father Basil did not set out to do anything particularly unusual or try to come up with any special insights. He did not talk or exhort a lot, although he did give short talks to the House called 'Jaws'. He was not much inclined to lay down rules, having no special liking for imposing his own personal views. Little interested in the exercise of control, he did not relish being an enforcer.

Corporal punishment was commonplace in private boarding schools at that time and used by both headmasters and housemasters. A number of former pupils have spoken, without rancour, of being beaten by Father Basil, but it is widely believed that he was uncomfortable with it and felt embarrassed afterwards. He sometimes may have preferred not to have to do it, but, at the same time, he would not have wanted to undermine the masters who sent boys to him for punishment. Sometimes he found ways of avoiding it, coming up with other means of handling the situation.

His approach to the job of housemaster, which probably owed more to instinct than any conscious deliberation or calculation, was to instil standards and values by being himself. He did not hold himself up as an example and expect people to follow; instead, he set himself high standards, inspired the boys to set standards for themselves, and then helped them to live up to those standards. He had many qualities which people found attractive, disarming and endearing. He was a likeable, engaging person, naturally charming. This influenced the effect he had on people. More importantly, as became increasingly apparent later, he was a holy man whose religious faith and monastic vocation were the most significant things about him.

His holiness was not apparent to all his adolescent charges at the time, some of whom say it went over their heads. Not all young people, struggling with the anxieties and self-absorption of adolescence, recognize the other-worldliness of others. Some, though, noticed a special quality. One, aged 14, went home at the end of his first term and said, 'I have had a very strange experience. I think I have met a living saint.'

Father Basil did not overdo the emphasis on religion or advertise his own spirituality. Nevertheless, worship of God was the basis of almost everything he did. His approach to the students was informed by it, and his instincts as a schoolmaster derived from it. He regarded all beings as God's creatures and he had genuine respect for the boys and their dignity. He saw his interests and their interests as largely coinciding and the boys consequently saw him as being 'on their side'.

A crucial quality he had, resulting from his religious faith, was that he was always able to see good in people. Consequently, he usually brought out the best in them.

He once said in an interview that he was a firm believer in the essential goodness of human nature. He trusted the boys – an approach which Father Paul Nevill had done much to foster – and showed confidence in them. This led them to develop confidence in themselves. He took pleasure in their individual efforts and loved it when boys tried even if they did not succeed. This was enormously encouraging for them.

He did not reach every boy, of course, which was a disappointment to him. Though this saddened him, he did not let it rankle and he never wrote anybody off. A few found him distant. Some believe that towards the end he was unable to devote enough time to the House because he had too many other roles within the school and monastery. They consider some of his boys may have suffered as a result. These, though, are a minority.

Several of Father Basil's qualities were invaluable to him as a schoolmaster. These included his honesty – he was a very genuine person – his fair-mindedness, kindness and helpfulness. He was able to empathize with the boys and show them understanding. Apparently, he saved one boy from expulsion on three separate occasions when the school authorities were advocating it. A former pupil recalls Father Basil asking him in for a gentle chat and saying to him:

You seem unhappy? Please don't think you have to explain anything but just let me tell you what I tell myself when things get bad. First, 'there is sense in this, no matter I can't see it'. Second, 'love is always stronger than fear'. Then he sent the boy to the dormitory to sleep.

Basil was a good listener, though he seems to have found it easier to put some boys at their ease than others. He was shyer than appeared on the surface and used to blush quite often. He probably found it difficult to approach boys for the first time without obvious cause and may have preferred to be approached. Nevertheless, he did have a gift for putting many individuals at their ease and for listening patiently. There often used to be a queue of boys outside his study at the end of the day waiting to chat to him. Often he would stay up late, if necessary, to talk to them. The more a boy was in trouble, the more attention he gave him.

His humility and simplicity were noticeable: he often used to ask senior boys, 'How did I do? Did they understand what I was trying to explain?'

Despite his simplicity, he was not above using innocent stratagems. He was very good at recognizing former pupils and old boys who had been in the school with him, but he was not infallible. When he failed to place somebody he would sometimes say, 'Forgive me but I have forgotten your name.' 'John Binks,' they would say, to which he would respond, 'No! No, I know your *surname*; I meant your Christian name!'

There were other invaluable Basil qualities. There was his awareness – he could be very astute and switched-on and he was wise. The boys thought him savvy, thought he had his feet on the ground. It amused them that while distributing the boys' mail he often recognized the handwriting on the letters, and, noticing an unfamiliar hand, would joke, 'Ah, a new girlfriend then?' Father Basil was astute enough to call someone's bluff. He could be firm – the boys knew where he stood on Catholic teaching. He himself recorded that:

> When I was a housemaster, some guys came to me and said that someone –let's call him Miles – 'had got some funny ideas – he doesn't believe Jesus was God'. This was in the late 1950s so I got hold of Miles and said, 'Miles, what you believe is your business, but this is a Catholic school and I have given up having a wife and family, all that because of my belief – that Jesus was God and your parents sent you to this Catholic school because Jesus was God. You can hang on to your opinions, all I am saying is you've got to be logical. You can't stay in a Catholic school built on the fact

that Jesus was God. There are four buses tomorrow.' And I gave him the timetable! He came back to me the next day and said that he had got over his doubts.

Basil Hume said that he could not have used the same approach in later years – the world had changed. Changes both in society and the Church meant such a blunt riposte to someone's religious doubts could not be used.

It helped that he had a good sense of humour. Once in a history class he mentioned that Henry IV of France 'had a long nose, and the strength of an ox'. The class laughed – Basil had a long French nose. 'What are you laughing at?' he asked, 'I don't have the strength of an ox.' On another occasion a boy disrupted his French class by whispering a joke to his neighbours. Basil asked him to see him in his study that evening. The boy feared the worst. When the time came, Basil sat him down and asked him to let him in on the joke. The boy retold it and Basil laughed heartily. The boy thought he had avoided punishment. But at the next French lesson Father Basil asked him to share the joke with the whole class, in French.

Father Basil's performance as a teacher in the classroom left some vivid memories. One former pupil recalls two stories which show his effectiveness as a teacher both of history and religion:

After completing our O levels in our first year, 12 of us were in Father Basil's European history one-year A level class. It was 6.45 p.m. at the first class in September 1958, when Father Basil bounced in with a used envelope and no books or notes. We stood up. 'Gentlemen, please sit' (for some reason he used this form of address to spotty 15-year-old potential historians, but not when we were in his religious instruction set).

'Gentlemen, you have a problem, which gives me a problem and that is that the wonderful men who are your fathers, thinking that like their fathers in the first war, they might well be killed in the second, found your wonderful mothers and had you lot. The problem is that there are far too many of you and so ... it is no good getting an A level, you will have to get an S [scholarship] level. The person who will give you an S grade is the marker of your paper. Why does anybody want to mark examinations? The answer is gentlemen they do it for the money – five shillings a paper. So, the person who is going to appreciate your papers the most is the marker who has the least papers to mark. He will probably be an Anglican vicar in Wales, who gets eggs in the offertory plate. Therefore gentlemen, we have to do the most unpopular subject on the menu.

I think I have come up with the answer: 'Swedish history and the Hanseatic league 1580 to 1720'. I know nothing and you know nothing, but I promise you gentlemen I will be 40 minutes ahead of you.'

He taught us brilliantly off the back of an envelope, prepared God knows how, in his unbelievably busy life as housemaster, First XV coach and theology teacher in the monastery. Ten of us got S level history.

At the same time he taught us religious instruction at 12.15 on Fridays. Once again he bounced in and asked if there were any questions before we started. Some idiot, not a historian, asked the most boring question possible in a monastic school.

'Please, sir, why do we have to go to Mass every day and twice on Sunday?'

The most obvious answer is the one given to a private by the company sergeant major. 'Why us Sarge?'; 'Because yer 'ere lad.'

Father Basil said, 'I will take the question and I will give you the same answer at the beginning and at the end. The answer is to give you the habit of it.' At this point he pointed to each one of us, saying, 'When the following happens to each one of you – you will go to prison, the girl will marry the other man, you will go bust, you will be killed in battle, you will be in a wheelchair, you will die young, you will have a long terminal illness, your children will get into trouble, your rival will get the promotion, unjustifiably etc. Not *if* but *when* one of these things happens to each one of you, if you don't find it a comfort to go to Mass and say a prayer in front of the Blessed Sacrament, some time in the next 25 years, I want you to come back and complain to me.

Now I will give you the same answer at the end. It is to give you the habit of it.'

There was total silence and did we ever pay attention to his wonderful discourses on the faith.

Father Basil worked hard at his teaching in class. At times he would write out a piece of work in an exercise book to show a pupil how it should have been done, perhaps 200–300 words in French. He was jovial in class, sometimes playfully throwing chalk at his pupils.

He also taught rugby. He loved the game and very much enjoyed coaching it. He was supposed to have told the boys that he always wore rugby shorts under his habit. He was a good motivator and very up to date, even ahead of his time, with tactics and technique, taking a keen interest in the latest training methods of the South African team. He used to say, 'It is the fourth ruck that scores the try, not the set piece.' To the boys' surprise he was really competitive about rugby and expected them to be. He used to drill the forwards 'mercilessly', but he always taught the boys to play cleanly.

While Father Basil was First XV rugby coach he warned team members of the dangers of London before the London tour, telling them that when he was in the XV the whole team had gone to a club called the Kit Kat Club. He said he was the only member of the team who did not end up with a girl on his knee. An uncomfortable silence followed. Father Basil and the boys seemed embarrassed. Then a member of the team asked, 'What is the address of the Kit Kat Club, sir?' whereupon everybody, including Father Basil shook with laughter.

Father Basil was often playful. As a former member of the XV recalls:

The First XV were on their way back from Coxwold where we had been celebrating the season now ended. Led by our Coach, Father Basil, we were a cheerful and high-spirited group as we cycled along the pretty valley road. 'Do you know, I used to be able to ride a bike backwards, sitting on the handlebars?' remarked Basil to nobody in particular. 'Could you really?', 'I don't believe it', 'I bet you couldn't do it now', 'Go on, sir' came the chorus from the First XV. 'All right then, watch me,' came the reply from Father Basil as he got off his bike, turned round and climbed aboard the handlebars. Putting his feet to the pedals, he gave an almighty thrust – and propelled himself straight into the ditch.

The First XV were quick to rally round their stricken coach. We picked him up, dusted him down, and continued back to school, slightly less boisterous now.

Boys being boys, Father Basil might have expected the story of his humiliation to have been round the school and into the monastery by teatime. But this was Father Basil and these were the First XV. We knew what we had to do and that is probably why this episode has not emerged until today. But it raised him in our estimation from coach to hero, and that is what he has always been since.

At Father Basil's House 'Jaws' at the beginning and end of term, there were several simple refrains. He would speak about the importance of saying one's prayers and the comfort to be had from it. 'When you put your pyjamas on, that is the reminder to kneel down and say your prayers. Just before you take your pyjamas off, that's the next reminder to say your prayers'. At an old boys' reunion he reminded them, 'If you get down on your knees in the morning and evening, you know you are going to be all right.' At the end of term he would advise the boys returning home: 'Your mother will go on treating you as if you were 8 years old long after you have left school. Mine does and I am the wrong side of 35. All mothers do. Don't take it personally. Humour her'. Another refrain was: 'Don't always follow the herd – try to think for yourselves; everybody has some things they can do well – everybody can make a valuable contribution.' Seen in cold print, 50 years on, this is unremarkable, but the fact grown men can still remember it so long afterwards suggests it was effective.

One remembers him speaking about prayer along these lines:

> Always remember that you don't have to kneel to pray. You can, and should, pray wherever and whenever you can. God is with you all the time so it matters not a jot whether you are sitting, standing, walking, in your bath or just doing nothing. So, next time you are waiting for a bus and wondering when, and if, one will ever come, say your prayers instead of fretting ... you'll be surprised by how quickly the time passes and perhaps at how easy it can be to pray when you are in a crowd. It helps to remind you that you, and everything and everyone around you, are God's creation.

Father Basil's faith and his personal qualities made him a born schoolmaster. Yet when he started, it is doubtful that he would have regarded himself as having a vocation for teaching. He became a schoolmaster as a result of his vocation as a monk. Teaching was a way for him to serve God at that time. His former pupils (and their parents) generally acknowledge that he had a major effect for the good on their lives. They consider they owe him a debt of gratitude. They have memories of him sliding down the steps on his heels in front of his house, of his bounding up the circular steps to his old room at the top of the clock tower, and of his having a go, kicking a football with the boys before the start of rugby practice.

They remember him with great fondness.

Monastic, Administrative and Pastoral Experience at Ampleforth

Abbot Patrick Barry OSB*

For 13 years before Basil Hume was appointed Archbishop of Westminster he served as Abbot of Ampleforth Abbey where he had lived the Benedictine monastic life for 34 years. It is not at all extravagant to suggest that his experience as abbot laid a foundation which was both spiritually and in other ways of vital importance for his future role in the Church. This conviction is far from the common stereotyped idea that his monastic experience was confined to peace and contemplation in the cloister in an environment irrelevant to the complications of the world he faced as archbishop. The truth is different and needs to be appreciated by those who seek an understanding of his life.

---

* Abbot Patrick Barry was headmaster of Ampleforth College from 1964 to 1980. Father Basil was abbot from 1963 to 1976. Their partnership during these years was very fruitful. Abbot Patrick was abbot of the community from 1984 to 1997, and joined Ampleforth in 1935. (*Ed.*)

There were at that time of his appointment as Archbishop plenty of media questions about his suitability for the job to which he was newly committed. There was a general assumption that he was unprepared by his background for such a demanding public position. ('Much too humble to make known his abilities. Could easily be missed!' was one media comment.) On the whole, he personally fared well in that early inquisition and quite rapidly, to the surprise of many, established as good a relationship with the media as anyone could have expected of a new archbishop.

During the following 23 years he was tested by problems on every side. In his position at Westminster he was inevitably seen by the press as leader of the Catholic Church in England. He was therefore involved in any public controversy which seemed to have a bearing on religion, and there were plenty of such disputes. It was a time of unrelenting, sometimes savage, trial for him in which instant responses were demanded about everything from the trivial to the profound. He had triumphs and embarrassments, but through them all his personal approachability and the sincerity of his faith earned him a sympathetic hearing. He emerged in public life as a figure of national importance and influence.

The widespread sense of loss at his unexpectedly early death and the warm appreciation in the media of what he had stood for in the nation as a whole were witness enough to his success. Nevertheless, woven into the accolades there were still occasionally expressions of surprise at how such an impressive public performance could possibly have emerged from so unpromising a background as a Benedictine monastery in the North of England and a Catholic public school.

It is the time, therefore, to look dispassionately at the actual truth of what that background involved for Basil Hume personally. It may even be possible to hope for a suspension of the ingrained English suspicion of monastic life and for a truce to the prejudices of those against independent education. Such a suspension of prejudice may open the way for an appreciation of the really positive influences in Basil Hume's monastic experience which were not irrelevant to his public life as Cardinal Archbishop but in fact did much to help him and prepare him for what was to come. I was personally involved with him during the latter part of that period and had plenty of opportunity to appreciate his growth in stature. Back in 1962 it was Father Basil who first made me aware of the possibility of radical change in both our lives, which would lead to other and more demanding responsibilities. Neither of us would have chosen such a change at that time, but he was more realistic than I and saw the encroaching signs before I did.

Father Basil at the time was a young Benedictine monk. After completing his theological studies in Fribourg, Switzerland, he had returned to his monastery at Ampleforth and joined the teaching staff of the school. After four years he was made housemaster and quickly became a popular figure in the school. He had a high profile in the games world as coach of the First XV for rugby football which made him especially popular with the game's players. He had a strong standing also in the monastic community through teaching theology to the junior monks and in the academic life of the school as head of the Modern Languages Department. On the whole, I think, he was at that time very happily fulfilled in a life of monastic prayer and devoted service as a gifted teacher of the young.

I myself had already been involved in various administrative responsibilities in the school, beginning as librarian in 1942 and by 1962 as second master, head of the Classics Department and housemaster. The death of my mentor, Father Paul Nevill, in 1954, eight years before this time, had been a blow for everyone. Father Paul had been headmaster for 30 years, from 1924 until his death. He had been my headmaster, who guided and advised me in my decision to become a monk in 1935. His influence was crucial in my life, as in that of many others, going far beyond what might normally be expected of a headmaster. For me, as for some others also, the loss of his example, advice, support and above all his presence and friendship had been devastating. By 1963 I had managed to get back on an even keel again in my vocation as a monk and in teaching, administrative and pastoral work in the school. I was content with my lot and was not looking for any more dramas in my life.

Father Basil, however, evidently had more antennae out in the large and growing monastic community. He told me one day in late 1962 that he and I were becoming front runners in the community for the office of abbot. I knew that in spring 1963 Abbot Herbert Byrne's third term as abbot would come to an end and there must be a new election. However, for many reasons I had confidently assumed that Abbot Byrne would be re-elected for eight more years. He had shown over the years a very steady Amplefordian habit of being re-elected, and was popular and manifestly successful as abbot. His record was very impressive. In spite of this, Father Basil now told me that there was a strong mood in the community for a change to a younger leadership and that many had their eyes on one of us. I remember him saying that, since in these circumstances we could not now talk freely to anyone else in the community for fear of electioneering, we had better talk to each other. And so began a strange and unforgettable period of daily dialogue between us as we discreetly escaped in free moments from gatherings of the community. In a long monastic life I have never known anything quite like it. We just had to get out of the way to leave others free to discuss what they thought of us.

I thought at the time that I knew Father Basil reasonably

well, but I got to know him much better during those days. He had joined the community some six years later than I, and by this time I had returned from Oxford and was deeply involved in school work. It was not until 1951 when he came back from his theological studies and joined the school teaching staff that our paths began to cross in the course of our school work. There was also an occasion when he was sent with me by Abbot Byrne to St Louis, Missouri, to the foundation we had made there in 1955. It was an episode of intense work and some delicate negotiations and we made a combined report to the abbot and Council. Now in 1962 he jolted me out of my complacency and I rapidly got to know him much better. I was glad of our association during the months that followed. I certainly learned to appreciate his great qualities better, but I also saw clearly that we were very different in temperament.

He was impulsive, generous, eager to talk things through, and he loved being at the centre of a group. He was gifted with the 'common touch' and loved to follow the fortunes of a favourite football team. This later impressed the media men as an aspect of the Cardinal Archbishop which struck a chord of understanding for ordinary mortals. He had studied theology in a mainline continental university at Fribourg in Switzerland. This was less appreciated by the media but was more important than football as a preparation for the role of an archbishop.

I myself was more cautious and analytic. I was not a loner, but I was always seizing opportunities to retire into the worlds of my primary personal interests in calligraphy, typography, stone-carving, printing and, above all, private theological reading. I had no favourite football team and was very deficient in the common touch, and still more deficient in the charismatic touch that seemed so important to many in those days. These were the diversities of temperament which would bring shared strength and on occasion lead to problems in our work together. I think we both appreciated the differences and knew we could not, and should not, attempt to change. It was never a question of a 'clash of personalities', although that and other clichés were at times invoked by others to explain our differences. In those days we spent together before the election I certainly understood our differences in a way that helped in the time to come. It was a time of learning and all of it in the context of our deeply shared Benedictine spirituality in a strong community of high ideals, to which we were both committed. Then, in April 1963, came Father Basil's election as abbot, and for a short time I thought that my life would return to something like its former rhythm; but it was not to be so.

MONASTERY

The newly-elected Abbot Basil was young for the job and not very experienced, but he rapidly won everybody's heart. It would have been wonderful for him and for the monastic community if he could have enjoyed a real honeymoon period of easing himself into the many new and demanding responsibilities with the avuncular assistance and advice of the now retired Abbot Herbert Byrne. However, this was 1963 and in those uncertain times such a calm and truly monastic transition was no longer possible. It was not only in the world of the community at Ampleforth that change was in the air and youth seemed to be taking over. The whole Church was in the throes of what proved to be a major upheaval in the aftermath of the Second Vatican Council, while in the school there were very urgent needs at several levels which called for far-reaching decisions. All such decisions now depended ultimately on Abbot Basil in his new role which, for the school, was equivalent to that of chairman of governors in other independent schools.

Abbot Basil was thus, with his monastic Council, responsible for the government of the school and faced with the task of meeting its needs. His responsibilities for the school were formidable enough, but the responsibilities he now shouldered stretched much further than the monastery and school at Ampleforth. He was now charged with the personal care of not only a community of over 120 monks of all ages, but also of some 20 parishes in northern England and Wales, St Benet's Hall in Oxford University and a priory and school in St Louis, which was still a dependent house, governed from Ampleforth. Then in addition to the government of the schools of Ampleforth College and Gilling Castle Preparatory School, he was also ultimately responsible for the governance of a number of primary and secondary schools in our Benedictine parishes. This brought him into contact with the Voluntary Aided Catholic School system, with the often controversial educational policies of the Catholic bishops of England and Wales working through the Catholic Education Council and the many conflicts of interest and aspiration reflected in the lively educational controversies of the time, which were far-reaching in their effects for the future. This and changing aspirations among Catholic parents made it ever more difficult for parochial schools to survive and combine a strong Catholic spirit with the sort of standards and options in education demanded by an increasingly articulate laity. The ultimate responsibility for dealing with these very complex issues in our parishes, which were incorporated in the monastery, fell on the shoulders of the abbot. It was a heavy burden but it also provided him with invaluable experience.

These pastoral and administrative responsibilities would have been demanding enough if the times had been tranquil, but they were not. The Church itself was developing under the impact of the Second Vatican

Council, which was coming to an end just at the time when Basil Hume became abbot, but it was in the following years that its far-reaching effects began to tell in the Catholic Church in England. Catholicism in the North of England was still at that time strong, secure in its beliefs and quite unprepared to deal with changes and new perspectives and initiatives affecting its treasured tradition. The North of England had suffered in many ways during and after Hitler's war, but it had not been involved in the radical uprooting which had done so much to disrupt life and challenge traditional beliefs on the Continent. Now quite suddenly Catholics were faced with changes in liturgy, practice and apparently in the Church's doctrine and outlook on the world, which seemed to contradict the very things which up to that time they had been encouraged to regard as sacred. The monastery itself was not protected from the turmoil and self-questioning that resulted, nor was the school. In the monastery and the community generally the problems fell heavily on Abbot Basil. He was a northerner himself with a strong historical sense of the value of tradition and continuity, and personally experienced the fundamental questions raised by Vatican II in the light of solid Benedictine tradition. The Benedictine concept of stability itself seemed to be under fire.

What was a personal problem for the rest of us was for Abbot Basil an agonizing sense of his responsibility for the whole community and for each individual in it. Religious life itself and many of the standards for living as a Catholic were under fire. In all this the community in the three facets of its life – in the monastery itself, in the school and on the parishes – was inescapably involved, each entangled in different problems arising from the turmoil of the times. The young abbot they had elected agonized daily about his role and responsibility. The monastery with its many varied works was in fact like a microcosm of the Church at large.

For Abbot Basil it was a trial by fire and he came through that trial with great credit to himself and great benefit to his community. It was a time when it became clear that many religious communities had been irrevocably damaged or virtually destroyed while many priests and many members of religious orders abandoned their vocations.

Ampleforth could not be immune from the spirit of the times. You cannot have the blessing of vocations and a substantial body of intelligent young monks in a large and ancient community, with its own firm and sometimes entrenched traditions, without, at such a time, feeling the tremors of the yearning for change which were becoming typical of the young everywhere in the West at that time. I will never forget those early years of Basil's experience of being abbot when, looking unusually pale and worried, he told me something of the yearning, discontent and incoherence of the younger members of the monastic community. They had found him a good listener, and lost no time in pouring out the mixture of idealism, scepticism, desire for they knew not what and anger looking for a target – the sort of anger that was fashionable and was coming to be regarded as the signature of the youth of the time. The title of a play in London expressed the essence of it: *Look Back in Anger.* Anger itself was the thing and the target was the past and those who represented it. For the young at Ampleforth it was not as bad as that, but the themes were the same and the young monks poured it all out on their new young abbot.

In response to our need to understand the Vatican Council, Abbot Basil invited Abbot (later Bishop) Butler, fresh from his work in the Council itself, to talk to the community. That for many of us was the most helpful light we had glimpsed regarding what was happening in the Church. It did not, however, lessen the disturbing effect on the community of some of the wild reports and speculations about change that were being spread. I remember Abbot

Basil saying to me one day how deeply he was concerned about certain wild notions concerning Catholicism itself and Benedictine life in the future that were finding their way into the community.

There were other problems in the community for the new abbot to face. As changes increased in the liturgy, monastic observance and the Church at large, the shockwaves were felt among the older brethren and the many monks serving on the parishes. For all of them there was the personal agony of facing unimagined change in their habits of mind and practice. There were many personal problems and some even left. All the personal anxieties and problems came to Abbot Basil and it was a marvel of his own perseverance and leadership that the community as a whole held together and suffered so few defections. The personal strain on him at that time was terrible and it is reflected in the portrait painted by Derek Clarke. Yet also reflected there, though with less emphasis, was the spiritual strength that saw him through with such benefit to his community.

I remember a day when I went to Abbot Basil specifically to thank him on my own behalf for preserving the essentials on which our future could still be built, when he could so easily have succumbed to the iconoclasm of the time. He was getting different signals from others in the community and, although he was grateful for what I said, I could see that his agony continued. I call it 'agony' because he was not able, and did not try, to stand back from the personal concerns of the individuals in the community. Later, when he became a bishop, he found it easier from this point of view, because he no longer had to live in close daily contact 'with his own mistakes'. That is how he put it with notable humility, but he might perhaps with justice have added that there was real consolation in living with his successes. It was still a strong community that he left behind him when he went to Westminster.

The invaluable experience of those years for Abbot Basil was not confined to the affairs of the school and monastic community at Ampleforth. Of course he was involved in meetings with other abbots in England, on the Continent and in Rome. We could tell how highly he had come to be thought of in this wider international forum, when he was requested by Rome to carry out a visitation of a large and well-known monastery on the Continent. He faced there a tangled and difficult situation. His recommendations were accepted and peace was restored on which the future could be built. At Ampleforth it was felt at the time that we were fortunate to have an abbot of such stature.

Abbot Basil's responsibility for the new foundation in St Louis took him across the Atlantic to make difficult decisions in a distant cultural ambience. He had to send some more monks to the USA from England. He had to travel over there to discuss its future prospects with the founding laymen and the resident community. During his first ten years as abbot, Basil Hume had many worries about the ability of the foundation to survive at all.

There had been in the beginning a just expectation of American vocations. That had been in 1955 and the Catholic world in America had changed more dramatically than in England. No satisfactory arrangement for the recruitment and formation of novices could be devised until the monastery became independent and more thoroughly Americanized. The foundation was saved in the end in 1973 through the heroic decision of Father Luke Rigby,[1] the prior of St Louis, and his community to accept independence and make it work on their own without any further help from

---

[1] Father Luke Rigby was the second appointed prior of St Louis Priory, succeeding Father Columba Cary Elwes. After attaining independence the St Louis community then elected Father Luke as their first abbot.

Ampleforth. They were rewarded with truly impressive success. It was a relief to Abbot Basil and he had surely learned a lot in those worrying ten years of trying to solve problems in the USA from a remote base in North Yorkshire.

SCHOOL

In the year after Abbot Basil's election, the earthquake of change at Ampleforth reached me. Abbot Basil had decided that I should take over the school as headmaster. The four terms since his election had been time enough for the shifting tectonic plates, moved partly perhaps by this major change in the monastery, to bring to the surface many urgent aspects of the need for change in the school. I thought I knew it all as second master, and I did have more than an inkling of what was to come. I remember already in the late fifties discussing with Father Denis Waddilove the need for big changes in the school. I had not, however, fully anticipated the strength of the tidal waves that were about to surge through the worlds of education and religious teaching of the young. Father Denis and I had seen and foreseen quite a lot from our position as housemasters, and our eyes were rapidly opened still further when I became headmaster and he second master. The initial result was inevitable. We began going to the abbot with our lists of major problems which awaited decisions and would cost money. He was not going to have a restful, easy time in the monastery, in the parishes or in the school. The stock image of a monk wrapped in a cloud of dreamy contemplation far away from the harsh world of work was not quite working out for him, even in his earliest days as Abbot of Ampleforth. Not much could be taken for granted in the developing life of the monastery and in the school it became increasingly clear that some very radical changes were urgently needed for mere survival.

As I took over responsibility for the school in 1964 it was ten years since the death of Father Paul Nevill. His 30 years of leading the community had been ones of steady growth in numbers in the school and increasing prestige. He was revered by old boys of the school, who had no doubts that his record was definitive and that his example must be followed exactly by whoever might succeed him. The older they were, and therefore at the time the more influential, the more certain they were that the key to the future was to cling to the solutions of the past. Already some years before his death they had begun to express doubts whether there was anyone in the monastery who could succeed Father Paul and preserve his legacy intact. They shook their distinguished heads and spread a sense of anxiety about the future of the school.

Father William Price was appointed headmaster in January 1954 and was faced with an unenviable task. In his ten years as headmaster he followed the policies of his predecessor, effectively maintained academic standards and guided the school with dignity and firmness. He even increased the numbers in the school by adding two houses. It was testimony enough of his success. However, it had been a time of containment and quite apart from the shifting demands on schools in society at large and in the world of education, there were some vital and potentially explosive issues which were waiting for solution by his successor.

The four most urgent of these issues were: the status and full involvement of the lay members of the teaching staff; the development of the curriculum to meet the rapidly changing needs of a new generation during rapid change and expansion in university education; the provision of adequate classrooms and other central facilities, to bring them up to date and catch up with the expansion of numbers in the houses; and the need to replace or refurbish some of the older buildings. It was indeed a formidable list calling for some radical changes, needing substantial new investment and active fundraising. No headmaster alone could solve these problems. The governing structure of the school would inevitably be severely tested in any attempt to deal with them. The monastic structure, which was all that existed at the time, depended heavily on the abbot personally, without any expertise from outside to call on.

Abbot Basil's responsibilities for the governance of the school at Ampleforth caused him many anxieties and faced him with the responsibility for decisions about policy and funding for which he had little preparation. He authorized an appeal for funds leading to a very substantial programme of building and renovation, and both the renovations and new buildings were much needed at the time. What was achieved made possible many later developments for the future of Ampleforth including the very important diversification of the abbey's pastoral and apostolic work. During his 13 years as abbot, on top of his other responsibilities, Basil never had much peace on the front of expenditure and development in the school. In that sense I did not give him an easy time with my requests and plans. However, he did understand the urgency of the needs and it was his support that enabled me to bring the school fairly well up to date and leave a viable structure, both physical and academic, on which further necessary developments could be built in the years to come.

The needs for the school at the time of Abbot Basil's election were inescapable. Under my two predecessors there had been rapid expansion in the numbers in the school for which boarding accommodation of a high standard for the time had been provided, but the updating and extra provision for teaching an expanding curriculum and facilities for games had been neglected. The abbot had to take ultimate responsibility for the many associated problems of planning and finance and he had the difficult task of carrying with him the monastic community. He was equal to the demands that were made on him and it was wonderful to be able to count on his understanding and support during that turbulent but creative period. At the end of our work together the school had been transformed and was in a strong competitive position. We were faced on the way with many difficulties and there were initial disagreements about the aims and pace of development. This was inevitable in times of much uncertainty in the world of education and a confusion of voices on the religious front. Yet somehow, with the strong monastic background to which we were sincerely devoted, we resolved our difficulties and the results speak for themselves. The changes and developments in the school over the 15 years I was headmaster and Abbot Basil equivalent to chairman of governors illustrate the wonderful support Abbot Basil gave me, the vision he shared with me and the important experience he gained himself at this time, as well as the value it certainly had for him as a preparation for some of the larger administrative responsibilities he was to assume as archbishop.

To give one example, the laity were increasingly to take a full part in the academic and pastoral responsibilities in the school. In 1964, when I took over as headmaster, the lay assistant teaching staff were still quite separate from the monks with their own common room and private organization. By tradition, they held no positions of responsibility (head of department, housemaster etc.) and were expected to work under the assumption that they were not much more than assistants to the monastic community in running the school. I privately discussed their situation and needs with two senior lay staff. What they told me made me more aware of their profound discontent and of the urgent need for action, I decided that I must act immediately. I spoke with Abbot Basil and told him of my plan. He gave his approval for immediate change and that was the beginning of many initiatives to which he gave his generous support. On this occasion my first act was to hold a full staff meeting (the first of its kind at Ampleforth) of all teachers – both monks and laity – in which I told them that from then on there would be only one staff and one common room for all who were teaching in the school. Abbot Basil's quiet support at the beginning and throughout the unfolding changes was absolutely crucial.

It must be admitted that we did not share exactly the same views about the educational controversies that were raging in the country in the sixties and after. He sympathized up to a point with my emphasis on academic excellence, but temperamentally he was attracted also to the egalitarian theories of the left, which were dominant at the time – that academic excellence could look after itself and that the thing to do was to crowd pupils of all abilities into the same classrooms. This attitude was well received in the world of the parishes where he was responsible for parish Voluntary Aided Catholic Schools. He was not the only one who never could reconcile the two policies but tried to hold onto them in theory, while practice inevitably drove them apart. I am all the more grateful in recognizing his unfailing support for my policy in the development of the school at Ampleforth. Many other examples could be given of Abbot Basil's understanding and support of development in the school during these difficult times.

Perhaps the most important point to be made in this connection is that through his position he came into contact with young students about to go to university, with their parents, and with many of the problems that faced them in the post-Vatican II Catholic world and the threats to Christian faith they faced in a spiritually degenerating society. There can have been few surprises for him in this area when he went to Westminster.

6

Farewell Chapter of Abbot Basil Hume
11 March 1976

On 17 February 1976, the Vatican announced that Abbot Basil Hume was to be the new Archbishop of Westminster, succeeding Cardinal Heenan, who had died in late 1975. Less than a month after the announcement, Abbot Basil left the Yorkshire valley which had been his home for almost 40 years. The night before he left, he gave a final address – a chapter – to the monastic community resident at Ampleforth.

> I cannot think of any less auspicious circumstances for giving a Chapter than the preparations which we have had in the last hour and a half [farewells to the staff], and the circumstances inevitably attendant on a moment such as this; but this is my last act as Abbot of Ampleforth.
>
> I want to tell you, principally, about the half hour I spent with the Holy Father [ten days' previously, on 1 March 1976, the archbishop-elect had been received in audience at the Vatican by Pope Paul VI] because, as far as I was concerned, this was a very transforming experience and I think that I can express much of what I want to say to you through that experience. It is very rare to be accorded a private audience under six or seven weeks' notice, and so I

counted myself privileged and lucky. When I walked into the Holy Father's room – The Library, as it is called – where he receives people in private audience, he started off in Latin with '*Benedictus qui venit in Nomine Domini*' ['Blessed is he who comes in the name of the Lord']. I don't know if he says that to everybody, but it was very impressive. Then he said three words in English: 'Welcome, welcome, welcome,' and then, 'Now we will talk in French.' So we sat down side-by-side and we talked for half an hour. By that time my French was beginning to come back. The interview was a very remarkable experience because he is without question a 'man of God', a man of prayer and a man of very fine spirituality. This was transparent, I thought, in his appearance and very much so in his whole approach to you, quite, quite different to the image one gets from reading about him in the press; he is a very remarkable man spiritually. And so immediately I felt at ease, at home, and so I said to him, 'Well, you are the Holy Father and I am going to open my heart to you.' I did precisely that. I told him what my fears were, what were my misgivings, and in what way my conscience was troubled. And I think that from the moment of that interview, as far as this present change in my life is concerned, I felt a different person.

There are four things amongst many memorable things which he said and which I told [our monks in the parishes] in Warrington last Monday. I told them that it was just exactly as if one was talking to Abbot Byrne, although he had not got the same kind of characteristic wit and edge of Abbot Byrne, but he had all the rest ... I told him that this was a situation which I found very difficult to accept, and I explained that a bit. Then he said, 'Well, remember the prophet Jeremiah,' and he quoted the [passage where Jeremiah expresses his own misgivings to God] and said that was always the authentic response to being given responsibility. And he said, 'It is my task to lay the Cross on the shoulders of other people.' Then he went on to say, 'Had you refused, you would have been refusing the call of Christ.' Now, in the context of that conversation and the person that one recognized as a man of God, quite apart from his position in the Church, that was a most amazing thing to have said to one – 'To refuse this was to refuse the call of Christ'. I only say that to you because I think that it will help you as it helped me. However good or bad your abbot is, the change of abbot is nonetheless a very significant moment in the history of the community, but to have that reassurance that this was the will of Christ, that it expressed the will of God, makes it very easy to accept. It had already been made clear to me in London [by the apostolic pronuncio], as I think I told you on a previous occasion, that I would not have been allowed to refuse. At that moment, as on other moments in life, one lives what I call the 'freedom of obedience'. It is a very remarkable thing to experience the freedom of obedience, where one's own preoccupations, one's own desires, affections, all that is important in daily living, becomes subordinate to obedience to the will of God. That is a freedom which is a liberation. It was at that moment that my whole attitude to what had happened changed. This was God's will; that was all that mattered.

He then went on to tell me that he wanted me to remain a monk. He said: 'You are a monk and must remain a monk.' But ... how does one see this appointment within the context of one's own monastic life? I said to the parish fathers on Monday: 'All of you are doing a pastoral job out of obedience. Some of you running youth clubs, some as parish priests, others with more specialized forms of pastoral ministry. I see myself as being sent out, just like you, to do a pastoral job; it happens to be as an archbishop in the South of England and not an organizer of a youth club in the North – just a fine distinction. But that is the way I see it: I am going out to do a job of work like you on the parishes.' This is very important for me, fathers, because whatever the niceties of the canonical position, it is unthinkable for me to see myself as anything but one of us. Both temperamentally and monastically speaking this is too important, too much part of me, too much part of my life, to think of as otherwise, and I hope you appreciate that point because without

69

wishing to get in the hair of my successor, or be in any way a nuisance, you must regard me as one of yourselves, whatever the canonical position. That is the way I see it. Tomorrow I go out on the parishes as many of our fathers have done over the years, out of obedience.

If you can bear with me; it is only once in a lifetime that one is allowed to be more personal than on normal occasions. Curiously enough, I find myself with no particular fears, no particular anxieties, and at one level of my being I am extremely shattered and sad, and terribly sorry to be leaving you, and all that that means. Nonetheless I cannot understand the freedom and peace which I am enjoying at the moment. It is temperamentally not me; I can only understand it in terms of an answer to prayers which you and many others are offering. You can only say that when you recognize that it is not your own achievement, but is the achievement of God through you at the request of other people. I simply cannot understand it, a remarkable gift to be given by the Lord.

I cannot say that I shall not cry all the way to Doncaster tomorrow; I fully intend to, and I have warned Father Geoffrey [who was to drive him to London]. But deep down I find myself at peace. If you will allow me to go even further: over the past three to five years I have known a darkness to life which I had never known before. I say this to you not to reveal myself, but as a way of encouraging you. I cannot understand that darkness, and it has been a great strain. I understand now more why it had to be; if you enjoy moments of darkness it is only because they are to be followed by moments of light and all that is in the hands of God. That is what life is like; it is an alternation between darkness and light, of high and low, good days and bad, the Cross one day, the Resurrection the next. I share that with you, not only as a privilege at the moment of departure but because it may help you. They have not been easy years, but in a remarkable way, before any announcement was made, things changed and that is the grace of God: '*Non nobis, Domine, non nobis, sed nomine tuo do gloriam*' ['Not to us, Lord, not to us, but to your name give the glory'].

... A monastic community is made up of a great number of very varied temperaments, of people with different strengths and weaknesses. In that context re-read the *Rule of St Benedict* and see what a brilliant document it is. The strong must always be given something to strive after; we must never arrange life so that the weak suffer. If any monastic community forgets that, forgets the tolerance it has to have for its weakest members, then it has no future, and in my opinion it does not deserve to have one. It is not because I am leaving, not because of the wonderful collation we were given, that I can say whatever our faults, whatever our weaknesses, whatever our historical circumstances, this is by any standards a very fine community.

... As I have said on a previous occasion, and which you must take as true, I would not be leaving you tomorrow if you had not done what you did in 1963. There is no question of it; it is not my person who has been selected, it is the Abbot of Ampleforth; there is a big distinction between the two.

I think, fathers, that with that I have said it all. It remains for me only to thank you for your loyalty, your affection and for all that I have been given by this community – after all I have been around since I was 10! There have not been many other formative influences. I think it only right, fathers, that in our monastic tradition that I should end by begging pardon and penance from you for all the hurts, misunderstandings and stupidities which have been mine in exercising the responsibility to which you elected me. God bless you.

7

A Historic Day at Westminster

Abbot Patrick Barry OSB

So, after 13 intense and demanding years as abbot, Basil Hume became Archbishop of Westminster. On that day, 25 March 1976, he was the central figure in two ceremonies, one in the morning and the other in the late afternoon. They took place at opposite ends of Victoria Street in London. The first was at the Catholic Cathedral of Westminster, in which the Pope's mandate was read out and Basil Hume was ordained archbishop in the course of a Solemn Mass and in the presence of the Westminster clergy, the Catholic bishops of England and Wales and many representatives, not only of the Catholic Church, but of the Anglican Church and also of other Christian denominations.

These ecumenical representatives are often referred to on such occasions as 'observers' but that word suggests a detached attitude which does not do justice to the strong atmosphere of joyful affirmation from everyone in the cathedral on that day. It is better, in all the circumstances, to call them 'friendly witnesses'. Apart from the religious witnesses, there were many others from every level of civil society including, of course, the publicity agents of the

73

media who were in an exceptionally friendly frame of mind. The whole ceremony was televised. It was an occasion on which the unusual appointment of a Benedictine abbot to the office of archbishop of the premier Catholic diocese in the country had attracted not only interest but great expressions of goodwill. His predecessor at Ampleforth, Abbot Herbert Byrne, was there, in spite of his advanced age, and I remember him with tears in his eyes calling down blessings on the new archbishop.

The second great ceremony was in Westminster Abbey. Archbishop Hume went there in response to the far-seeing invitation of Dean Edward Carpenter, the dean of the abbey. The consecration ceremony in the cathedral had been the routine and ancient beginning of a Catholic bishop's dedication to his diocese. There was no precedent for the other ceremony which followed it in Westminster Abbey. That was unique and it was clearly inspired in a generous spirit of ecumenism by the fact that the new Archbishop of Westminster was a Benedictine monk. The abbey had been founded by a holy Saxon King for the Benedictines and it had for more than five centuries from its foundation been a centre of Benedictine prayer in London. Then for four further centuries from the time of Elizabeth I, although no longer Benedictine, it had remained very specially under exclusive royal patronage and had become a sacred place, now in the Anglican communion, for the crowning of kings and queens of England and for the burial and memorials of some of the country's more outstanding artists, writers, armed defenders and politicians. It was a great attraction for tourists, but by and large its Benedictine origins and purpose had been relegated to the remote background of forgotten history, although there always remained a persistent and eloquent reminder for those who visited the well-preserved monks' cloister which still spoke to the present of that past of Benedictine prayer.

Now on the day of Archbishop Basil Hume's consecration the dean had invited him to gather monks from his monastery at Ampleforth, who were joined by others from all the other Benedictine abbeys of England and by some distinguished Benedictine abbots and monks from abroad, to celebrate the daily monastic office of Vespers (evening prayer) in the abbey. For a moment of vivid significance Westminster Abbey was restored on that occasion to the purpose for which it had been founded so many centuries ago. The Benedictine monks were united with the Anglican dean and chapter on that day in the ancient monastic evening prayer of Vespers which had been ordained for them in the *Rule of St Benedict*. Thus it happened that from a large choir of Benedictines the haunting and prayerful music of plainsong rang again through the whole abbey. The event attracted a huge congregation in the nave, which included Catholics and Anglicans and many who were simply interested to see an unusual occasion, including casual tourists and sightseers who just happened to be there at the time. The abbey was so full for that celebration that there was no room for more when the doors were shut.

There was no sermon as such, but at the end of Vespers, Dean Edward Carpenter spoke briefly in a personal message of warm welcome to Archbishop Hume. He said that at the time of the Reformation, 'only a prophet could have foreseen that the voices of [the Benedictines'] successors would rise again within these walls'. He then referred to what he called the abbey's 'unique and intimate connection'[1] with the

---

[1] The reference is to a lineal connection between the Benedictines of Westminster Abbey, the Ampleforth community and whole English Benedictine congregation. This arises from a solemn and documented act in 1607 whereby the last surviving Benedictine of Marian Westminster passed on the monastic habit to two young Englishmen from whom the present Ampleforth and whole English Benedictine congregation have developed through the ages.

Ampleforth community. 'It is good for us,' he said, 'that they should be here together with some of their brethren from other monasteries.' He saw in this 'a call to look together to the future'.

Archbishop Basil Hume's response was equally generous. He thanked the dean warmly for making this great occasion possible by his ecumenical vision and manifest readiness to work for mutual understanding. He then made everyone – including the press – sit up and attend by a quite unexpected reference to two Tudor queens who had been in the forefront of the bitter clashes between Catholics and Protestants in the sixteenth century, when mutual detestation had been the order of the day and there was no question on either side of ecumenical outreach. Having referred to the ancient wounds of division which Catholics and Anglicans in England bear in their hearts, he went on to refer to one of the royal tombs in Westminster Abbey:

> which contains the remains of two sisters, Elizabeth and Mary. Read there the inscription: 'here we rest, two sisters, Elizabeth and Mary, in the hope of one resurrection'. Think of them as you will, judge them as you will, but pass on in your mind to the last phrase 'in the hope of one resurrection'.

This led him to sound what became a keynote of his time as Archbishop of Westminster. He called for work together in the hope of achieving reconciliation between Anglicans and Catholics. He borrowed a phrase from Pope Paul VI by referring to the two Churches as 'sister Churches'. This was a fearless way of leaving no one in doubt about the ecumenical ideal he wished to pursue. It was in this way that the Anglican dean, who had invited him to the abbey, and the new archbishop himself, made abundantly clear their hopes for reconciliation and unity. In their words they emphasized two essential factors which must be in place, if the vision, to which both referred, were ever to become a reality. Prayer – and specifically prayer together, based on their shared baptism into Christ – must be the foundation. Secondly, in an age of compromise we must search unashamedly for truth. Archbishop Basil's words on this point were: 'It must be a courageous, relentless and honest search for what is the truth about God and his purpose for man.' Those words also had a touch of the prophetic, both in the sense of prediction and of warning, as we began to enter the age in which an intellectual fashion grew up of justifying everything by the denial of the existence of truth.

But there was more to that solemn prayer together in the abbey and it is worth some consideration. It arises from another important point about the Benedictine Vespers on 25 March 1976. It is a point which should be quite free from controversy and it is vital for reconciliation. In the first place, that ceremony of Solemn Vespers in Westminster Abbey was a strong reminder of the relationship between Benedictine prayer and Anglican liturgy. The Benedictine framework of worship has always, since St Benedict's day in the sixth century, been the antiphonal singing[2] or chanting of psalms, antiphons, hymns and other scripture-based prayers. It was this framework that gave shape – in the context of the former monastic cathedrals – and much of its spirit to the new Anglican liturgy of the Prayer Book. To some Anglicans present when the Benedictines sang the ancient Office of the Church, there was a sudden appreciation of the link. This occasion for them seemed to be not an alien intrusion but a moment of family recognition. There was for them something of a sensation of coming home.

---

[2] A form of singing where a choir, in groups of two or more, sing phrases alternately.

Curiously enough for many of the Catholics who took part, it was equally a moment of recognition. There had been in England a decade of serious ecumenical development among Catholics which had brought forward some truths formerly neglected or obscured by controversy. There was, for instance, the point that sincere prayer together in the light of common baptism actually achieved true unity before God, during the time devoted to such prayer. It might be a transient unity but it was very real. It was an experience which undoubtedly left its spiritual mark on many of those who sincerely took part in it. It did not dispose of nor deny the importance of serious differences in teaching and the interpretation of the Gospel. Nevertheless it did for the moment actually bypass those differences and achieve a unity brought to life in the presence of God. Too often, both before Westminster and since, ecumenical approaches have focused primarily on the Eucharist. Of course that is the centre, but the best approach to it is through the actual experience of unity in non-Eucharistic prayer by those who are otherwise divided but united in their common baptism and faith in Christ. This was the key to the experience of many in that congregation in the abbey and it was not illusory nor, though temporary, was it lacking in lasting power and significance.

In fact the publicity through the media on that very special occasion inspired, on more ordinary occasions, many who had not been there. It opened the gates, which had so long been shut, to similar momentary unity in prayer all over the country. There was a significant revival of prayer together between Catholics and Anglicans. In many of the cathedrals and old Benedictine churches monks were invited to sing again the plainchant of the monastic *opus Dei*. In my personal experience, without any great publicity, congregations were crowded with ordinary people on such occasions. It may have seemed to some a piece of romantic antiquarianism. Well, even if there was a touch of that about it, the more important point was that Anglicans and Catholics were praying together in momentary but profound faith in real unity before God. That was a very significant experience for many ordinary people and it was the sort of ecumenism of which we cannot have enough.

To understand this aspect of Benedictine Vespers at Westminster and much that followed it, and to understand also the spirit of Benedictine ecumenism it may be helpful to reflect on some aspects of the Benedictine vocation. After all, it was Basil Hume's response to that vocation as a young man which ultimately led to the occasion at Westminster and to his far-reaching commitment to ecumenism. To gain some understanding of this vocation one needs to appreciate that Benedictines are not dedicated primarily to external good works, whether of the apostolate itself or of caring for others. Some of them have undertaken such works in all ages; some have given themselves more or less exclusively to prayer, silence and solitary study. All Benedictines of whatever observance have been united in seeing that their primary obligation is to the celebration of daily prayer in community. That daily prayer is the expression of our worship, gratitude, repentance, love and praise of God through Christ our Redeemer in the Holy Spirit. It is so special and important for monks that they celebrate it together in the monastic choir with intercession for all in need. When that is clear it is easy to see why St Benedict called it the *opus Dei*, that is the 'work of God' and insisted that it should come first in a monk's life and that nothing whatever should be put before it. It is important to recognize that such daily community prayer was always understood to be the participation in, and a vital contribution to, the prayer of the whole Church, which is modelled on the prayer of Christ in the desert and on the mountain and in Gethsemane, the garden in which He spent the night

79

in agonized prayer before being taken prisoner and executed on the Cross.

Now on this great occasion in Westminster Abbey there were many with a strong sense of history who remembered that the origins of Christianity in England were monastic. In Kent, the mission of St Augustine from Rome brought the faith not in the first place (as St Bede describes it) by going out to preach the Gospel but by very simply living the life of monastic prayer, which drew the people in to learn more of the Gospel. In the North also it was the Celtic monastic ideal of Iona – through St Aidan, St Cuthbert and St Wilfrid – that brought the Gospel to the people of Northumbria. With the Normans of the eleventh century it was monasticism again that prevailed as a prayer-centred ideal for monks. So strong was this influence that England was unique in Europe with its nine monastic cathedrals, including Canterbury, where Benedictine prayer had been the inspiration of the diocese since St Augustine's time. During Vespers in Westminster Abbey on his inauguration day, Archbishop Hume undoubtedly thought back to this tradition of handing on the faith through monastic prayer.

Monastic prayer is community prayer, so there was a personal sense of loss for him in the move to a rather solitary and isolated life at Westminster. That change is a sacrifice which any monk must accept if he is called to the episcopate. The loss of daily community prayer for a Benedictine is a serious spiritual change. The loss has been felt by countless Benedictines who through the centuries have been called to serve the Church as bishops. Pope St Gregory the Great, who was himself a monk and sent St Augustine, another monk, to England, felt it acutely. On one occasion he lamented the loss eloquently and feared for his own soul when he was called to the papacy and found himself burdened with 'the care of all the Churches' that deprived him of the quiet and contemplation of his monastery in Rome. It was widely recognized that Basil Hume in the course of his service at Westminster, though similarly deprived by his elevation, found ways – like Pope St Gregory – to preserve in spite of everything the central sense of prayer, quiet and meditation in his personal life. Especially towards the end of his life as Cardinal Archbishop it was recognized by many – even journalists, publicists and 'men of the world' – that, when they met him on direct personal terms as well as in many of his public pronouncements he communicated a sense of prayer and holiness. There are many public testimonies to this quality in him. Although he had lost the form of Benedictine prayer and dedication, he had learned through many trials to preserve the inner reality. The key – which was symbolic but also much more than symbolic – to that deep union of inner prayer and outward service of the Church and many beyond the Church, was brilliantly expressed at the beginning in that ceremony in Westminster Abbey.

When he came to that ceremony, Basil Hume did not wear his new purple robes of an archbishop. He came in his monastic habit and looked very much at home in Westminster Abbey. The theme of that afternoon was undoubtedly ecumenical. It was a theme that had been well integrated into his life as a monk. The spirit of the Abbey of Ampleforth in the wilds of North Yorkshire had something of value, in this respect, to offer the South.

When Archbishop Hume returned after that ceremony of solemn Benedictine Vespers to the forbidding residence, called Archbishop's House, at the other end of Victoria Street, he was alone as he had never really been before. He was faced with a task of such complexity and so personally demanding that it might have appeared not formidable but impossible.

PART TWO

Cardinal-Archbishop

8

Basil Hume the Pastor: Westminster Recollections

In clerical gossip circles today one occasionally hears something along the lines of 'Father X will never be a bishop, he hasn't got enough parish experience'. The implication is clear: strong, pastoral leaders are required, and the real place to gain the necessary pastoral insight and skills is in the parish, at the coalface. If this were true, if significant parish experience were essential to climbing the ecclesiastical ladder, and if this applied in the mid-1970s, then Basil Hume's appointment to Westminster in 1976 is all the more remarkable, for he had limited parish experience. However, that does not mean to say that he was not a great shepherd of the flock entrusted to his care.

He may have been too young to appreciate fully what he saw, but some of the incidents already referred to from the early 1930s made a lasting impression on the 10-year-old Basil Hume, in particular seeing some of the poorer areas of Newcastle when the Dominican priest, Father Pike, took him on his rounds of visits. The comparative affluence of Ellison Place was a far cry from the poverty of the Shieldfield and Byker areas of Newcastle. As the late

Monsignor Kevin Nichols wrote, Basil Hume 'came to see children without shoes, and families living in a single damp, comfortless room. He was able to sense the atmosphere of misery and hopelessness' (*Pilgrimage of Grace*, Veritas, Dublin 2000, p. 8).

Undoubtedly it may be a cliché, but this sense of a shepherd visiting his needy flock had a tremendous impact on Basil. So when, probably sometime around 1939–40, he was thinking about a religious vocation, the fact that Benedictine monks of Ampleforth were working in 20-plus parishes was of great importance to him. He could become a Benedictine monk and still have the opportunity to work with ordinary people at a parish level.

For the next ten years, however, the novice and then monk spent most of his time devoted to study, first of all in Ampleforth itself, then at St Benet's Hall in Oxford (1944–47), and finally in Fribourg, Switzerland (1947–51), where he studied theology. Father Basil returned from Fribourg in the summer of 1951. He had been a priest for a year, and in September 1951 he was to get his first taste of parish life when he was appointed assistant priest in the Catholic parish of Our Lady and St Benedict in Ampleforth village. The parish priest was 40-year-old Father Hubert Stephenson, who had taught in the school since 1935 and had been appointed parish priest during Basil's time in Fribourg.

The young 28-year-old curate soon became very popular and Father Basil is well-remembered to this day. His duties included preparing the 7-year-olds for their first confession and first Holy Communion and it was done with such success that first confession was not approached by the children with some degree of fear and trepidation, but a degree of knowledge that this was an opportunity for forgiveness from the Lord. Even outside confession Father Basil became the receiver of many childhood confidences.

Much has been written about Basil's role in rugby

coaching at the college. What is less well-known, perhaps, is that he would often spend time during the holidays coaching children from the village on the college sports fields. But it wasn't just having fun for the sake of having fun – behind the play and the laughter was the serious side of this young monk. In the midst of all the fun there would often come a punchline based on some experience currently causing problems within the group of children. With hindsight, someone once said, 'You realized he had a direct line to God.'

Speaking about his time in the village, Basil himself said that he looked back on the appointment:

> with unmitigated joy. It was all so new. Sunday Mass with sermon, weekly instruction in the primary school, in full charge when the parish priest was absent, the people – yes, especially the people, teaching me how to be a pastor, very significantly their goodness and faith put me to shame ... It did not last long, for other appointments in the monastery and the school took me away from the priestly ministry in the village. I was genuinely saddened.

Alongside his parish duties, Basil Hume was already teaching in the college and fulfilling a number of monastic roles. And perhaps inevitably his work in a parish, something that had helped sway him towards the idea of becoming a Benedictine monk, was soon to come to an end. In 1955 he was appointed a housemaster of St Bede's House.

Much is made in schools today, and rightly so, of the importance of the pastoral role of staff, with pastoral tutors, etc. and while over 50 years ago there may not have been such an overt pastoral emphasis it is clear that, for many of those who passed through his house, Basil Hume is remembered above all for what today would be seen as 'being pastoral'. For eight years as housemaster of St Bede's,

Basil was to demonstrate the pastoral skills and sensitivities he had begun to develop in the Ampleforth parish.

At this stage, Basil Hume was housemaster, Senior Modern Language Master and coach of the rugby First XV, and professor of dogmatic theology for the monks. Although opinions differed about him as a teacher ('good but unremarkable', some have said), as a tutor, guardian, mentor and role model he was exceptional. As one student said: 'He had a very special quality: he always seemed to be able to see good in people and to recognize the hidden value in individuals. As a consequence, he brought out the best in them.'

Deep down, Basil was a firm believer in the essential goodness of human nature. He perceived the foibles of the human condition but was a man of deep kindness. Many of the students from St Bede's House remember Basil Hume above all as a friend, somebody whose humanity and humility touched them. His Monday night talks to the House – 'Jaws' as they are still known – were inspirational and punctuated with sound pastoral advice: 'Be your own man', 'Avoid the herd instinct', 'Don't take yourself too seriously'. But, like the young parishioners in Ampleforth village, many of the young students, too, would seek out Basil to talk to him in confidence, to pour out their troubles. In St Bede's House, seeing students waiting outside the housemaster's study was not normally a sign of impending punishment.

The ability to provide a listening ear, a firm belief in the goodness of human nature and being on the lookout for those in trouble or need: Basil Hume may have had limited direct contact with the 'ordinary people' in parishes, but all these pastoral qualities came to the fore in the many diverse situations he encountered first as monk and then as Cardinal Archbishop.

Two stories from his very early days in Westminster

indicate very clearly the pastoral insight of the new archbishop. On his arrival in the diocese in 1976, one of the first things he did was to ensure that all the priests of the diocese had his private telephone number, a phone that only he answered: 'Call me anytime,' he said, 'for I am there for the men who are with the people.' The sign was very clear: he was available to them at any time. Many of the priests carried that number with them all the time. When one priest in the diocese committed suicide, the young curate in the parish rang the Cardinal's phone number. The Cardinal went to the parish immediately on hearing the news. His concern was not only for the deceased but also for the impact such a tragic event might have on a newly-ordained priest. He spent some time with the young priest and at the weekend it was the Cardinal himself who in effect acted as the 'supply priest', celebrating Masses in the parish and providing a listening ear and a pastoral heart as news of the tragedy spread. As one priest reportedly remarked, for the parishioners and neighbours, 'the Cardinal was Christ walking beside them'.

The other story from the early days in Westminster is less sombre. In *Pilgrimage of Grace* Kevin Nichols recounted that, 'when Cardinal Hume came to Archbishop's House and sat down to his supper, he found the door leading to the house where the other priests lived, locked; and himself eating in solitary splendour. He sent for the key and joined them' (*Pilgrimage of Grace*, Veritas, Dublin 2000, p. 21). Here was an archbishop who wanted to be with his fellow priests, his co-workers.

More than 40 years after his first real glimpse of the effects of poverty in his hometown of Newcastle, Basil Hume was to see much of the same in and around the streets of Westminster. His secretary, Sally McAllister, recalls later in this book how she went into work one December day in 1980 and told the Cardinal how sad it was to see young people lying in sleeping bags in the snow. The Cardinal immediately went to go out and look for them and the Cathedral Hall was opened for them (which upset some of the neighbours). This temporary night shelter operated for two years before moving to new premises and in 2005 The Passage celebrated the 25th anniversary of its foundation by Cardinal Hume and the Daughters of Charity of St Vincent de Paul. Today, it runs London's largest voluntary sector day centre for homeless people, helping more than 200 homeless men and women each day and providing accommodation for more than 60 people. In October 1986 the problems of homeless young people in particular became the focus of the work of The Cardinal Hume Centre located not far from Westminster Cathedral. Since its establishment, it has set up a family centre, a medical centre, hostel accommodation and an education project.

These projects and more are testimony to the Cardinal's pastoral concerns. At the opening of a hostel at The Cardinal Hume Centre in 1989 he himself stated:

> Living and working in the centre of a city one cannot but be affected by the sight of the homeless on the streets. They are almost an expected feature of life in a big city, and it is tempting to think there is little or nothing that can, or even should, be done about it. This is not so. My interest in homelessness stems from the Christian obligation to help those in need. Our Lord says in St Matthew's Gospel: 'Insofar as you did this to one of the least of these brothers of mine, you did it to me'. So I believe that we have a duty to look frankly at the social conditions around us and do what we can to address the specific needs which we find.

In fact, in his 1993 book *Cardinal Hume and the Changing Face of English Catholicism*, author and journalist Peter Stanford recalls that the Cardinal once revealed to him:

If I weren't in this job, and if I weren't a monk, I should like to do something like run Centrepoint [a central London hostel for the homeless]. I feel very deeply about young people pouring into London at risk. I say constantly this is where the Church should be, this is our job.

(*Cardinal Hume and the Changing Face of English Catholicism*, Geoffrey Chapman, London 1993, p. 99)

To say the Cardinal would give the homeless the clothes off his back is almost literally true. One of the nuns who worked in Archbishop's House once gave a poor man a pair of the Cardinal's trousers. 'Heh,' the man said to the Cardinal some days later, 'do you know I'm wearing your trousers?' Basil didn't mind at all – but he did ask the nun to remove his name tape before giving away the next pair.

The poor and the homeless on his own doorstep had a profound impact on Basil Hume; bigger still was the impact of the starving people of Ethiopia, images of which filled television screens in October and November 1984. Basil himself often recounted why he decided to go to Ethiopia at that time, as, he said, an 'ambassador for the hungry'. Speaking to young people in Archbishop's House at the end of October 1984 he said:

I, like you and very many people in the nation, was sitting watching the nine o'clock news. I saw those pictures, and, like everyone else, was absolutely horrified because I knew, and others knew, that this was a situation in many countries, not only in Ethiopia. But to have that brought right into our sitting rooms was really quite terrifying. But, like so often with these things, it makes a tremendous impact, then life goes on. I think what was important was that we had it again the next night, and I have an idea that those pictures made a far greater impression than those on the previous night – certainly on me. Perhaps it was accumulative, and I sat there looking at those pictures and said to myself:

'Hume, there you are, sitting in an armchair watching this going on – little babies with flies on their faces, dying. Terrible.' And I really felt the world was upside down, and almost felt that my life was upside down.

Basil had had a good supper, too, and he became 'haunted', as he himself said, by a number of biblical passages: Dives and Lazarus, where the rich man, Lazarus, ends up in hell, while the beggar Dives enjoys eternal life; the Good Samaritan, which he reminded the young people was about 'the chap who got beaten up and the priest, the Levite, walked by and it's the Samaritan who comes to his help. I said to myself: "Hume, are you that priest walking by? What are you doing about it?"'; and the story of the Last Judgement, when those condemned plead 'But when, Lord, did we not feed you? When did we not clothe you?' and receive the answer, 'Whatever you do to one of these my little ones, you do to me.' Basil explained to the young people: 'I suddenly saw on my television screen, in that old man, in that woman, in that child, the face of Christ, waiting to be served by us.'

Speaking on the BBC after his return from Ethiopia, Basil explained how moved he was by what he had seen: 'It's one thing,' he said, 'to see the suffering and dying on the television screen and quite another to be there and experience it. You cannot look into the eyes of a starving child and yourself remain the same.' For the rest of his life, Basil had on the walls of his office a photo of a starving child, looking out hauntingly. He recalled:

> I [remember] a small boy who rushed up to me and took my hand and rubbed it against his face. He put his fingers to his mouth to show he was hungry; he just had a little loin cloth round his waist. He wouldn't let go of my hand and I thought to myself: 'This child is craving for food, craving for love', and in a very simple, direct and uncluttered way I

realized once again the fundamental needs of human beings are simple: the need for food, just to live, and the need to love, to be valued.

Ensuring that people knew they were valued was at the heart of Basil's pastoral nature. He was very generous in his estimation of people, especially those in difficulties, and would do all he could to be of help. This generosity of spirit, this willingness to always see the best in people, was at the heart of Basil's pastoral nature, guided, as ever, by the *Rule of St Benedict*. Speaking in 1995 to an international gathering of clergy he enunciated the principles from the *Rule* which, he said, guided him in whatever pastoral oversight he had:

> [the Superior] should always let mercy triumph over judgement so that he too may win mercy. He must hate faults but love the brothers. When he must punish them, he should use prudence and avoid extremes; otherwise, by rubbing too hard to remove the rust, he may break the vessel. He is to distrust his own frailty and remember not to crush the bruised reed. By this we do not mean that he should allow faults to flourish, but rather, as we have already said, he should prune them away with prudence and love as he sees best for each individual ... Therefore, drawing on this and other examples of discretion, the mother of virtues, he must so arrange everything that the strong have something for which to strive, and for the weak nothing from which to flee.
>
> (RSB 1980, 64.9, 15,19)

Nothing to flee from because, as Basil often indicated, every human being is loved by God. One of his favourite scripture passages was the series of parables in Chapter 15 of Luke's Gospel, focusing on the lost sheep, the lost coin and, above all, the story of the Prodigal Son. In this latter in particular Basil saw a revelation of what we mean to God.

He often encouraged people to reflect on one verse in the story of the Prodigal Son, when the father rushes out and embraces the long-lost son who is returning. Basil said:

> Our Lord is revealing to us what God is like. Deep down every human being is in need of human love. I want to be somebody's first choice, and I think the only one who knows me completely, understands me entirely, and wants me unconditionally, is God – and I am his first choice; and you are his first choice. The marvellous thing about God is that He cannot have second choices. He is limited that way! We are all first choices ... all the time, whatever my mood, whatever my attitudes, whatever my failures, I am his first choice.

Throughout his life, Basil Hume attempted to convey the idea that each person is God's first choice. He provided the listening ear, the open heart, the healing gesture. He himself made people feel valued, important, the only person who counted. 'I think one of the most important qualities,' he said, 'is to be able to say, even on bad days, the sort of "Hi" which invites further dialogue, rather than that "Hi" which is: "I want to go past rather quickly".'

It was precisely this deeply pastoral attitude which had an effect on so many people. Each person had potential, for they were God's first choice. Basil's pastoral outlook and concern for other people was not some quaint social skill, but something rooted firmly in his own faith and his awareness of God's call to sinners. From his early days as abbot to his final years as Archbishop of Westminster he often reflected on Jesus's calling of Matthew, the hated tax-collector (Mt. 9.9–13), and in particular the phrase, 'Those who are well have no need of a physician, but those who are sick ... For I have come to call not the righteous but sinners'. He once called this 'the most golden sentence in the whole of the Bible' – although there were others, too, that he sometimes referred to in the same way! Basil compared the humble tax-collector who knew he needed God to the Pharisees who trusted themselves and didn't think they needed saving. Speaking to his own community at Ampleforth he once said:

> They had missed the whole point. You, my dear brethren, and I can so easily live through life missing the whole point. You think that because you don't find prayer easy, you think that because attendance at Mass is something which is not congenial, you think that because your record in the service of God is not a good one, then the things of God are not for you. Can't you see that the more inadequate you are, the more you need God's help? You and I are not likely to make the mistake of the Pharisees. We are not likely to say 'I don't need to be saved', but we are likely to get into a frame of mind whereby we say 'I don't want to be saved', and when a man reaches that he has reached a sorry state. There is a yearning in me for security and happiness, half-conscious, unconfessed, yearning, although I don't know it, for God. It is this which Almighty God wishes to use. My heart will always be restless until it rests in Him. 'I have come to save sinners, not the just' – that, my dear brethren, means you and me.

As pastor Basil strove to show people how much they meant to God, the God who sent his own Son, Jesus, to save them. The positive impact that Basil Hume had on the lives of many people is testimony to his pastoral sensitivity and instincts. What is clear is that for him pastoral concern was part of his monasticism, not an added extra. Speaking to the monastic community in the mid-1960s, he quoted a French abbot who had said: 'The true monk is the man who, while living apart from the world, has his heart in the midst of the masses'.

And yet who knows if the heart of this monk tired of

being in the midst of modern society. When he arrived in Westminster there was a surge of enthusiasm and a number of new initiatives, a gentler, more pastoral approach to the management of the diocese than had previously been the case. In later years, and possibly as a result of disappointments, he was less adventurous. He felt public life had become coarser and wondered whether people had really been led to God. He had grown tired and was perhaps even out of sympathy with contemporary culture: 'Is this what we have created?', he wondered. In an address which he was scheduled to give in Washington on 25 June 1999 – the day of his funeral – he noted that often:

> what should be seen as icons of God's loveableness and beauty become idols which we worship ... pleasure; power; sex; wealth. It is these that can make us indifferent or even hostile to divine realities. The seed, the instinct for God which is part of our human make-up, withers and dies.

As his illness took hold, he could in fact no longer read or pray, nor even celebrate Mass or receive Communion. 'All I can do,' he said, 'is just sit here and look at this crucifix.' He found comfort and meaning in the words of Jesus himself on the cross: 'Father, into your hands I commend my spirit'. In his last days, that was his only prayer.

The week Basil Hume died, he was due to give two major addresses in America. In each of them, he quoted Pope John Paul II's reference to the need today for heralds of the Gospel who: 'are experts in humanity, who know the depths of the human heart, who can share the joys and hopes, the agonies and distress of people today, but are at the same time contemplatives who have fallen in love with God'. Many years earlier, he had spoken about the conflict within a novice entering the monastery, struggling to become humble and obedient. Then, he said, he will begin 'to run with unspeakable sweetness of love in the way of God's commandments' [RSB 1980, Prologue]. It will have dawned on the novice that God has at last found him, and made him his very own. He is now at peace.

The monk who had fallen in love with God and spent his life showing others that God loved them, too, was truly at peace.

9

Young People's Evenings

Teresa de Bertodano

Every person I meet is in some way superior to me. Each one can do something that I cannot do or knows something that I do not know – even if it is only the way to fix the television!
Cardinal Hume to a group of young people

Shortly after Cardinal Hume's arrival in Westminster in 1976 he received a visit from Jean Vanier, founder of the l'Arche communities for people with learning difficulties. There was a passing resemblance between the two tall men. When Jean was leaving for Archbishop's House with his sister Thérèse, a priest friend warned her: 'Make sure you bring the right one home!'

During their meeting, Jean Vanier and Cardinal Hume spoke of the needs of young people. The Cardinal told Jean that two young men had already been to see him to talk about the young. Jean suggested that the Cardinal consider inviting a group of young people to come and talk to him regularly. There would be no agenda apart from the sharing of thoughts and ideas. Jean mentioned some names including mine.

In due course I received a letter from Cardinal Hume's secretary, Father John Crowley. John suggested an initial meeting between himself and some interested young people. He came to supper in Thérèse Vanier's flat to meet Shelagh Lindsay from London, Una McCoy from Birmingham and myself. We liked the idea of coming to see the Cardinal but were a little unsure. How should we address him; how should we behave in the presence of a cardinal? John looked at us very seriously: 'You must come into his room on your knees – and backwards!'

The meetings began in 1977 with three girls and the two young men who had originally visited 'Father Basil' – the form of address he obviously preferred. The Cardinal claimed that he had said to the two young men: 'Come back and see me again – and bring some girls!'

'Father Basil' usually sat in the armchair in his study and we sat around on the floor. Conversation ranged widely and it soon became apparent that no holds were barred. Cardinal Hume made it clear that he did not want a meeting for 'found sheep'. 'The only qualification for coming to these meetings is that you should not have been to church for a year!' Some had not been to church at all.

The group included members of the international Focolare movement, which is inspired by the Gospel to work for unity in all spheres of life. By 1978 the meetings had become too large for the Cardinal's study and we adjourned to the 'Throne Room' next door – there was no alternative. We met once a month on a Saturday evening. Meetings began with tea and biscuits in the Throne Room. We then moved into the less imposing reception room which would be crammed with over 100 young people. Their ages ranged from early teens to the late twenties. The Cardinal would start the meeting by raising something that was on his mind or a subject on which he wanted feedback. We sometimes divided into 'buzz groups' for half an hour or so and the groups would 'feed back' to the larger meeting. We would end with prayer. As Cardinal Hume said: 'You may not like the prayer – but the tea is very good!'

One of Father Basil's greatest gifts was the sharing of personal difficulties in a way that made listeners feel, 'Perhaps I am not such a fool after all.' He described these and other experiences as 'theology for the eleven minus', and explained his reasons in a book based on the meetings called *Basil in Blunderland* (DLT, London 1997, p. 7):

> there used to be an examination called the 'eleven plus' . . . We used the term 'eleven minus' to indicate those who had not passed the 'eleven plus' examination . . . If you had passed your 'eleven plus' exam, then you had no place at my talks. You were probably too clever.

On a number of occasions Father Basil referred to a story he had been told as a child, also related elsewhere in this book. A small boy had gone into the larder and seen a large pile of apples. He knew that he was not supposed to take an apple and nobody was there to see him. But there was one person who was always watching – and that was God!

> It took me 40 years to recover from that story. For many years, I thought of God as somebody who was watching me all the time to see if I was getting it right, and catching me out when I got it wrong. It was not until I became Abbot of Ampleforth that I discovered that God was the sort of person who would nudge me and say 'take two apples'! God is always watching us but it is because he loves us so much that he cannot take his eyes off us.

Sometimes the young people's group would be joined by visitors staying in Archbishop's House. On one occasion the visitor was the West African Cardinal Bernardin Gantin from Benin. Someone raised a knotty problem. Cardinal

Hume pointed across at Cardinal Gantin. '*You* deal with that one!' Cardinal Gantin was not to be drawn. He shook his head vigorously and pointed back at Cardinal Hume who had to deal with the difficulty.

At one meeting a young man complained: 'My mother is always telling me what to wear and what to do.' Cardinal Hume advised that the problem was insoluble. He shared a personal experience: 'I was living in this house as a cardinal and my mother came to stay. Over breakfast on a cold winter morning she asked about my plans for the day. I told her where I was going. She said: "It's going to be very cold today. Make sure you wear your warm overcoat!"'

A minibus-load of riotous young people came from the Midlands every month with their chaplain. Unbeknown to their priest, the boys decided to explore Archbishop's House and collect 'souvenirs'. Their horrified chaplain discovered the 'souvenirs' on the journey home. The ringleader was sharing out the loot and included the priest in his bounty: 'Have a cigar, Father!' Cardinal Hume had been aware of the 'souvenir hunters'. He did not complain until a subsequent occasion when the boys raided the rooms belonging to the sisters who looked after Archbishop's House. The Cardinal banned the minibus group from the following meeting but made it clear that he wanted them back in the future.

On another occasion a young man accused the clergy of 'hiding behind their dog collars'. Cardinal Hume pulled off the offending collar and chucked it aside.

One of my 'collapsed' Catholic friends agreed to come to a meeting 'as long as the Cardinal doesn't wear all that scarlet and stuff'. I assured her that we had never seen him in 'scarlet and stuff'. The next meeting took place on a very hot summer's day. The Cardinal arrived slightly late. For the first time he was wearing his scarlet cassock! His smile disarmed my friend and he began with an apology: 'I'm very sorry to be dressed like this, but I can't take it off because I'm not wearing much underneath!'

During one of the meetings a girl asked about the presence of women in the Church: 'How many women work in the Vatican?' Cardinal Hume quipped back: 'None I hope – no, but seriously, I'll come back to that one later.' The meeting proceeded and he was unable to return to the subject. His remark rankled. I wrote a letter enquiring how he would have responded if the question had been: 'How many Jewish people work in the Vatican?', or 'How many Irish people?' At the next meeting somebody made a point with which the Cardinal obviously agreed. Instead of addressing the person who had made the point he looked across at me and gave what I took to be the answer to my letter: 'It is important that the right things are said. It doesn't matter who says them.'

By the early 1980s an occasional 'all day' gathering was added to the monthly Saturday evening meetings. Then we spent two days together. Lourdes was mentioned. What about a young people's pilgrimage to Lourdes? That was the start of the annual Young Adults Pilgrimage (YAP). Several coachloads of young pilgrims took off from Archbishop's House, crossed the Channel and thundered down the motorway towards Lourdes. Cardinal Hume encouraged the driver of the coach in which he was travelling to overtake all the others.

YAP became a regular fixture and had a powerful effect on the pilgrims. Cardinal Hume was very much at the heart of it. The young loved 'Father Basil' and he loved them back. They trusted him because they could see that there was no 'gap' between his words and his actions. He spoke as he lived.

Friendships were created and many young people discovered in Lourdes a spiritual reality they had never experienced in their own parishes. The smooth running of

YAP was to a large extent dependent on the cooperation of the rector of the Sanctuary of Lourdes. During a YAP pilgrimage in the late 1980s Cardinal Hume invited the rector to join the YAP pilgrims for lunch in the hotel. We stood behind our chairs while our soup cooled and Cardinal Hume expressed our gratitude. We anticipated an equally long 'thank you' in English. When the French 'thank you' was finished the Cardinal gave his 'translation'. 'I just said "thank you very much!".'

On the same pilgrimage the young people wanted to buy a present for him so they had a collection. On the final day they presented their gift – a simple gold bishop's ring to replace the ring presented to him by Pope Paul VI which had been stolen. The gift was completely unexpected. 'Father Basil' began to express his gratitude but was so deeply moved that he became unable to continue. He bowed his face into his hands. One of the priests began a hymn. Cardinal Hume gathered himself together, stopped the hymn and continued to say 'thank you'.

The meetings in Archbishop's House continued into the 1990s. I cherish the memory of a deeply human man of God who was not afraid to share the ups and downs of his spiritual journey with humour, with humanity and with deep simplicity:

> No one prays easily at first, just as I think no one really enjoys the first glass of beer. You've got to get used to beer, then you get hooked on it and want more and more! Prayer is like that. You have got to get hooked but at the beginning it is hard going!

Those Sunday evening meetings and the Lourdes experience have been among the greatest gifts I have received. I shall always be grateful for the privilege of being a participant.

10

Colleague and Friend

Sally McAllister

Shortly after the Cardinal died, as I stood in his room in St John & St Elizabeth's Hospital, I thought back over years of daily meetings. The longer I worked for him, the more I became aware of the heights and depths he lived; moments full of energy and light; times of hidden pain and dereliction. 'Shared weakness binds more than shared strength,' he had once told me.

The warm sunlight flooding his hospital room that day and the muffled sound of London traffic could not overcome the silence and stillness of death, but the knowledge that he was now enjoying the 'endless now of ecstatic love' about which he spoke with such eloquence, in some way tempered the loss and disbelief that he had finally gone.

The personal meeting with the One in whose presence he had lived for so long came quickly at the end. Now the man who described 'judgement' as 'being able to whisper into the ear of a loving father the story we had never been able to tell anyone', was able to tell his story and who knows what a loving embrace awaited him beyond the dark passing of death?

I began working in Archbishop's House, Westminster, in September 1978 and when shortly afterwards the

Cardinal's secretary was killed in a road accident, I worked for him while prospective secretaries were interviewed. When he offered me the job, it came as a complete surprise, not only because I hadn't applied for it but also because I still had a few years to go to reach the lower age limit of 25. With an earnest look which betrayed just a hint of vulnerability, he urged me not to take the job if I were doing it only for the love of God and actually found him a hideous person to work with. Nothing could have been further from the truth. Those years were, for me, a deeply formative experience.

Work was busy, never dull and constantly new. As the years went on, the volume of work increased quite considerably as he took on more responsibilities in Europe, particularly during his lengthy presidency of the Council of European Bishops' Conferences, and during the Synods of Bishops in Rome. Yet, I think his pastoral heart was most at home in his ministry in the diocese, and in ecumenical and inter-faith dialogue.

Particularly in his latter years, his favourite way of working on a text was to read aloud what he had written. When he asked for an opinion, I learned fairly early on to be very careful about what I said because he listened so very seriously. More often than not, it wasn't necessary to say anything; he already understood what could usefully be changed. He was a wordsmith, delighting in crafting, refining and redrafting until he was convinced he had managed to convey the nuance of the message, while maintaining the rhythm of the language.

And yet, some of his most original and inspiring work was not the polished texts but the spiritual insights which were the fruit of his life and which in turn touched the lives of so many. Ever the master of the 'one-liner', he could turn round difficult situations with real flashes of genius. At one ecumenical gathering he coined the phrase, 'not strangers

but pilgrims', which immediately became common cur-
rency, giving new impetus at a time when it was really
needed. He was not beyond experiencing real pleasure in
moments like that because although he did not react well to
flattery, he did need encouragement.

As his energy diminished with age and illness, the calls on
him increased. He met them with the same generosity with
which he did everything else. Until a few weeks before his
death he insisted on opening and reading all his mail
personally. Not only did he want to keep his finger on the
pulse but he was convinced that if he gave up that direct
link with the public, people would start hiding things from
him. Here I must say that in all the time I worked for him I
was never aware of anyone deliberately or successfully
keeping something from him. He was not as other-worldly
as he sometimes appeared.

One thing was certain: his conviction that every letter
coming to his desk should receive a response and be dealt
with quickly and courteously. He was particularly attentive
to those who were not well off, not well educated, not used
to mixing with cardinals and bishops. During his illness he
hoped the great and the good would understand that he
could not reply. But one type of letter which was given
particular attention was that which began – 'I have never
written to a Cardinal before ... ' In the weeks before his
death it pleased him enormously to be told that we were at
least attempting to acknowledge the sackloads of mail
reaching the house from well-wishers.

A few days after he announced his illness he received a
letter saying,

> You have accepted your illness and you are at peace ... I
> learned I was terminally ill the same day as you made that
> announcement. I am far from happy – I am frightened and
> I am angry and I am especially angry with you because

everyone will pray for you – but no one will pray for me – a lapsed Catholic who is divorced ...

By return of post the Cardinal replied: 'Don't ever say no one will pray for you for from this day on I will pray for you every day'. The response came back just as fast: 'I was so ashamed when I read your generous letter ... I was angry and bitter, forgive me'.

Among his last letters were those to people who had at times hurt him, sometimes publicly. Each letter was full of respect and love, every one a healing gesture to those who would neither have expected nor, I suspect in their own opinion, deserved it.

Cardinal Hume was not without his critics. One criticism was that he didn't consult enough. I suspect on one level that would have surprised him, because he was so sensitive not only to what was said but to another's silence. Yet, on another, it would not. A significant part of his formation was monastic. The idea that he was the abbot and work was done according to his timetable never really left him. That meant working up until the last postal delivery on Christmas Eve, and trying to achieve the virtually impossible task of taking holidays while he was on holiday, yet having to be in the office in his absence. When I once tried to explain the impossibility of this position, he responded with a winning smile and a cheery, 'that's right'. It was a lost cause.

It has also been suggested that he had a problem with women. I know he valued the contribution of women in many, many sensitive areas in the Church's ministry. He sought their advice through the normal consultative processes but also a great deal in private, too. He had a couple of women whose judgement he trusted, whom he consulted often. I think he didn't have a problem with women who didn't have a problem with him.

Plate 1. The young Mimi with Madeleine in 1920.

Plate 2. William Hume, father, at home in Newcastle c. 1937.

Plate 3. The young Humes with their cousins on the beach in Wimereux in 1926. (Back row, from the left Philippe de Villamil, Christine, Madeleine, George and Frances. Front row, Christiane and Nicole de Villamil.)

Plate 4. The future Cardinal (on the right) on the beach in Northumberland in 1960 with members of his family including Mimi (back row, second from left), his sister Madeleine (third from left), cousin Nicole (fourth from left). Kneeling on the left is his brother John. In the centre front is the editor with a football, sister and cousins.

Plate 5. Brother Basil on the day in September 1942 he made his simple vows, with sisters Frances and Christine (back to camera). Probably the most significant day of his life, when he committed himself to the monastic life.

Plate 6. Father Basil during his time as Housemaster in the 1950s.

Plate 7. Abbot Herbert Byrne. One of the three greatest influences on the future Cardinal.

Plate 8. Father Basil the day he was made Abbot. The group is standing outside the Abbey church above the entrance to the vaults. Left to right, John, Madeleine, Christine, the new Abbot and his mother.

Plate 9. Abbot Basil Hume. The portrait referred to in Abbot Patrick Barry's chapter on Abbot Hume at Ampleforth.

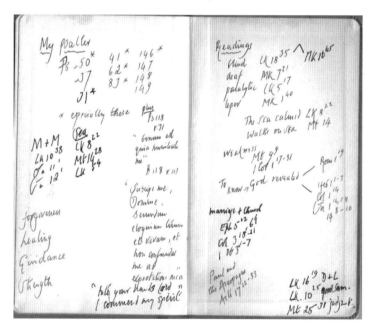

Plate 10. The Cardinal's psalm book, back pages. His favourite psalms and prayers are listed.

Plate 11. Cardinal Hume with Pope Paul VI in May 1976 on the day he was made a Cardinal.

Plate 12. Cardinal Hume on pilgrimage in Lourdes in July 1993.

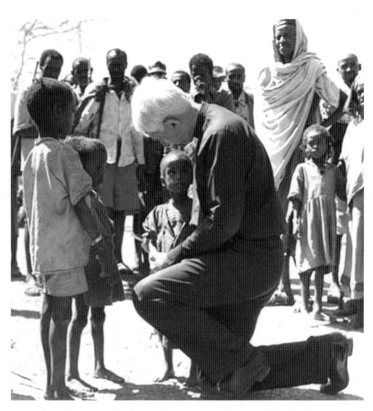

Plate 13. 'Each Christmas I call to mind my visit to Ethiopia.'

Plate 14. Cardinal Hume pleasantly surprised to see his family as he left Buckingham Palace after receiving the Order of Merit.

He loved a joke – often at his own expense, but never at the expense of anyone else. He maintained his sense of humour to the end. He was sharp, intuitive, able to see through sham. He wore well-darned pullovers and socks but recognized and appreciated 'good things'. Speaking of someone who should have known better and was fairly scruffy on a particular occasion, he once told me: 'Let's just put it like this – she wasn't dressed for the enclosure at Ascot!'

Most gifts he received were redistributed to those in need or to those who would appreciate them. That often gave more pleasure to him than the gift itself. At Christmas and Easter when cards arrived with money or cheques, he would rub his hands with glee, keep a careful tally of what he received and then divide it up and give it away. Perhaps my singularly most successful gift to him was a football key ring which emitted a loud cheer when squeezed and then played the theme tune from *Match of the Day*. For days the sound echoed round the corridors of Archbishop's House as staff and visitors were surprised by the noise of the key ring in his pocket which he pressed when no one expected it.

On learning of his illness he said that he wanted to die with nothing and so he began to give away the little personal money he had. He carefully made a list of everything, giving very clear indications of how it should be divided up. At his request, on the day he died, I withdrew the last money from his account, leaving it exactly as he wished: completely empty.

The heart of this great man was deeply pastoral. He had a particular gift in presenting issues around sexual morality. He always recognized the ideal to strive for but recognized, too, that people did not always meet that ideal. With boundless mercy and gentle encouragement he gave many the courage to start anew.

Arriving at work one wintry December day I said how

109

sad it was to see young people lying in sleeping bags in the snow and he immediately left the work we were doing to go out to look for them. His compassion and concern were not limited to personal gestures but resulted in his involvement in setting up agencies to help the homeless.

In the last years of his life he was plagued by bouts of depression and as a result became quite demanding and irritable. He agonized as to whether matters had been handled correctly, whether the correct form had been followed. Sometimes he required matters to be totally revisited and put to rights if necessary. His brother John's stroke was a sadness to him, making him wonder if the same would happen to him. He worried about what the future held for him after Westminster. It was not an easy time.

On occasions he would ring in the evening to talk over something he was particularly worried about, but the following morning would say nothing about the previous evening's discussions.

His sensitivity enabled him to see through to the heart of people and recognize the anguish of those tormented by doubt or depression. He stood alongside them in their dark night, not offering solutions but suggesting that when prayer was impossible, they, like him, might simply kiss the crucifix and repeat the words of Jesus from the cross: 'Father, into your hands I commit my spirit'. The Seven Last Words of Jesus from the cross were a favourite theme for his Lenten meditations but he confided that they had truly given up their meaning to him, particularly in his last weeks. The prayer of the good thief and Jesus's response were the Gospel reading he chose for Vespers following the reception of his body into Westminster Cathedral. I felt there was a special poignancy as I read the ending of that text 'and with these words he breathed his last' (Lk. 23.46).

With the diagnosis of his illness, the physical cause of his anxiety became clear. His 'dark night' over, the depression lifted and he found peace again. It was also a time when there was a 'healing' of relationships as well.

One relationship which needed no healing was that with the Palace. The day that he went to receive the Order of Merit from the Queen he knew he was dying: he also came back to Archbishop's House for the last time to say goodbye to the staff. On that occasion we spoke privately, at length. He spoke of his death, now imminent, which he faced without fear, even welcomed. It was a chance to say goodbye – and thank you to each other for all that had been in those 21 years. It wasn't the last time that I saw him alive but one that will remain for ever in my memory as a truly resurrection experience.

He was a mystical soul who reminded us all that we are made for the vision of God. To see Him as He is, face to face. A vision I am sure he is enjoying to the full.

11

The Steadfast Pilgrim

Bishop John Crowley

St John of the Cross enjoins his readers, 'If you want to be loved, be lovable'. Cardinal Hume was not only a much respected churchman but he was also greatly loved, as became increasingly apparent throughout his years at Westminster. He died in June 1999, just a few months short of the third millennium into which he had hoped to lead his diocese. Among the hundreds of letters which flooded into Archbishop's House after his death, there was a remarkable common feature: a great number of those who had never met him thought of him as a personal friend.

His family and those close to him knew how lovable he was from their own personal experience. But what was it that enabled the Cardinal to connect so deeply with people he had never met? How was he able to reach out in such a personal way to those whose only contact with him had been through the media, or through his writing and preaching? Perhaps it was in part something to do with the fact that he was a monk: a man from a completely different way of life to most of us, who was nevertheless able to make us aware that God was not only real but also accessible.

To a great extent the reality of being a monk defined

Cardinal Hume's spirituality. His monastic life helped to shape the human being he became after long years of submitting himself to 'the school of the Lord's service' within the daily rhythm of monastic life. He emerged onto the national stage in 1976 from a different background to that of the generality of diocesan bishops. Cardinal Hume had not come up within the diocesan system, therefore he was not seen as an ecclesiastic, someone who belonged primarily to the hierarchical institution.

The fact of being a monk does not necessarily make a person modest, unassuming or humble. But the Benedictine tradition does encourage these qualities: it perhaps helps to explain the reason why this monk cardinal won so many hearts outside the Roman Catholic Church as well as within it.

Basil Hume had a gift for friendship. Public gestures of affection were not to his taste, but in private he related warmly and spontaneously to those who meant much to him. He was steadfast in his prayer life, in good times and in bad. The former Abbot of Ampleforth, Timothy Wright, stayed in Archbishop's House early in 1999. He tells us that he was very moved by the fidelity with which Cardinal Hume was at his prayers early each morning, despite pain and debilitating sickness. Such persevering courage in the face of suffering provides another window into understanding how this man was able to reach out so effectively to many, many people through his writing and his speaking. For those who had to face their own struggles with pain or inner anguish, his was an *authentic* voice speaking to their experience. His words rang true.

An acute sense of fairness and a concern for the 'underdog' led Cardinal Hume to embrace many issues of social justice at home and abroad. Ethiopia retained a secure place in his affections from the time of his visit there during the 1984 famine.

The plight of the London homeless was a source of constant concern. He was conscious of his own more privileged background, and quick to throw his influence behind any initiative which sought to redress deprivation and social alienation. One specific legacy of his 23 years at Westminster is to be found in the various agencies dotted around Central London which reach out to those on the margins of life. Two obvious examples are the day centre, The Passage, and The Cardinal Hume Centre for young people and for families

A quality which endeared him to many, not least to the young, was his lively sense of humour – even of the absurd. Cardinal Hume was totally without pomposity, mixing easily with people of every background. Reassuringly for the rest of us, he was not without his faults. He did have a temper and on occasion could be autocratic and there were other failings and human vanities. But he spoke to his generation as few others could, and in a way which connected to those in any walk of life. It is not difficult to understand the great affection in which he was held. He was much loved because he was indeed very lovable.

Looking back across the ten years since his death provides us with a timely chance to review some aspects of his rich spiritual legacy. During his life he taught us how to love. Many commentators remarked on this and also on the fact that the manner in which he approached his death taught us how to die. Cardinal Hume had to face spiritual and physical suffering during the last period of his life as his general health deteriorated. The significance of this fact has not perhaps been sufficiently emphasized in the public accounts of his life.

In preparing this chapter I had the good fortune to have sight of what Sally McAllister has written in Chapter 10. Sally reflects upon the many years during which she came to know Cardinal Hume at a profound level as his personal secretary. Her experience is unique, not least in its longevity. Throughout the Cardinal's 23 years at the helm in Westminster, private secretaries who were priests came and went with regularity – six of us in all. Sally witnessed at first hand virtually the entire sweep of those years at Archbishop's House, beginning with the 53-year-old monk's arrival in London as the Ninth Archbishop of Westminster, and ending with his death from cancer in the London Hospital of St John & St Elizabeth in June 1999 at the age of 76.

At the time of his appointment, Abbot Hume was largely unknown on the national stage. By the time of his death he had secured a place in the affections of very many across the nation. Throughout the course of those years Sally McAllister had daily access to the man who did so much to change for the better the general perception of the Catholic Church in these islands. Her reflections offer a valuable new dimension to our understanding of Cardinal Hume as a private person holding down a high-profile job.

Reading what she records has certainly added to my own appreciation of someone I came to know well during his first years at Westminster. During the subsequent years when I was away from London, there were lengthy periods without regular contact. Sally's relatively short chapter helps to bridge a gap in my understanding of the Cardinal's inner journey. Her affectionate portrait is hugely appreciative, yet she does not gloss over the struggles, the vulnerabilities, the human frailty. These were particularly marked during the Cardinal's later years when physical suffering and, at times, considerable anguish of spirit led him along a steep upward path. It was a 'last lap' which needed considerable courage. The story of the Cardinal's final years perhaps finds an echo in aspects of the life of Mother Teresa, details of which have only recently come into the public forum. Previously unpublished documents make it clear that for much of her religious life Mother Teresa endured an almost total darkness in her spiritual self – a prolonged dark night of the soul.

What Sally has revealed has made me look in a fresh light at some of the incidents that occurred during my own time as private secretary (1976–82). This was the period of the Cardinal's first and formative years at Westminster. On the eve of his ordination as archbishop – 25 March 1976 – he gave an interview to the former religious correspondent of *The Times*, Clifford Longley, and spoke openly of the long period of inner darkness he had faced while he was Abbot of Ampleforth. This had been an experience which marked him deeply, leaving him with a profound empathy in subsequent years for those who suffered anguish or aridity in their faith. It left him with a sensitive understanding of those who were strongly tempted to abandon all belief in God.

Like every other human being, Cardinal Hume had to come to terms with loneliness down the years. He enjoyed the company of those close to him, and had a real gift for friendship with both women and men. There was a human warmth about him which encouraged affectionate relationships. He cherished his family ties, keeping them in good repair as best he could and he related easily and happily to the younger generation of Humes. Throughout his Westminster years he was much in demand for family baptisms and weddings, but he was no stranger to loneliness.

For him, its particular shape was that of a celibate who could in other circumstances have found deep fulfilment and solace within marriage. Occasionally he gave a hint of this hidden ache in the comments he made, although he was generally guarded in his public statements for fear of being misquoted or taken out of context. Although he felt things deeply and could be quite emotional in private, he was much less inclined to reveal his inner feelings in a public way. But on one occasion, when he was talking about his life, he said how much he missed the sense of being *uniquely* held in someone else's affection. His faithful prayer life gave him a lot of resilience, but it could not of its nature provide the same kind of emotional intimacy as, for example, a good marriage.

I remember him telling me that, on his first Christmas Day in London, when all the public duties were over and everyone else had gone home to family or simply disappeared from view, he wandered across to the upper library of Archbishop's House and cried there like a child for sheer loneliness.

A big challenge to the Cardinal over the years was the gradual loss of his physical fitness and, with it, the lack of the vigorous exercise he so relished and needed. On his arrival in London at the age of 53 he was still athletic in build, and keen to keep himself in good shape. In those early years he took determined measures to maintain fitness, playing squash regularly, or jogging around a nearby park. Several times a week he would also try to get out for a decent walk. Apart from the enjoyment it offered, such exercise provided a kind of therapy; a release from some of the tensions of his ministry. Hip and other health problems, allied to increasing age, drastically curtailed such outlets and the deprivation was sharp. It may well have been a contributory factor to the bouts of depression he apparently experienced during his later years.

To my knowledge, Cardinal Hume suffered less from anxiety and depression during his early years at Westminster than towards the end of his life. But there were nevertheless a number of occasions, even then, when he would use a kind of shorthand to indicate that he was under stress. He might simply say to me, for example, 'Don't worry, but for the time being I have flipped my lid.' When that happened he would try to lie low as best he could amidst the daily demands of such a high-profile position.

During these times of anguish he sometimes spoke of the consolation he received in slipping along to the house chapel to kiss the hands of the statue of Our Lady. Being shy of publicly expressed emotion, he always used to check beforehand that the coast was clear.

A real empathy for those under stress was characteristic of his approach. He was particularly sensitive to signs of strain in those who worked closely with him. On one occasion in the mid-1980s, after I had moved on from being private secretary to being Vicar General for Priests, he became aware that I was under strain in my work. He immediately 'ordered' that, until things righted themselves, I was to be dispensed from the daily recitation of the breviary. Knowing his man, he took great pains to help relieve the pressure-cooker building up inside me.

His sensitivity to those who were struggling at the sharp end of life led him to the barricades in some unexpected ways. During the 1980s the Holy See issued a document on homosexuality, the general tone of which was, in the Cardinal's judgement, alienating for people who were homosexual, and for many others. In places its language was rather harsh and insensitive, something that disturbed him greatly. Apart from issuing his own pastoral notes on the document, he was prepared to take up the cudgels in Rome itself. At the time I was a newly-fledged bishop making my first five-yearly *ad limina* ('to the threshold of the apostles') visit to Rome in the company of other members of the English and Welsh hierarchy. The key meeting on our agenda was at the Congregation for Doctrine and Faith, presided over by the prefect of the Congregation, the then Cardinal Josef Ratzinger. Cardinal Hume had great admiration for Cardinal Ratzinger, appreciating especially his fine theological mind and his immense courtesy and charm. This did not prevent him from engaging in some plain speaking exchanges with the Congregation's prefect.

His concern, he said, was not with Church teaching on homosexuality as such, but with the apparent lack of sensitivity and understanding shown in the language of the document. It was a fascinating insight into the tension Cardinal Hume not infrequently experienced during his years at Westminster, the tension between his frustration at the power play, the politics, and the sheer institutional shortcomings which are never far from the surface in Church affairs – and, on the other hand, his loyalty to Rome. That loyalty was underpinned by a strong Benedictine sense of obedience and by his personal admiration for Pope John Paul II.

A quality which is often mentioned in regard to the Cardinal is humility. It was an attractive feature of his personality which appealed to those of all faiths and of none. Cardinal Hume never gave the impression of being someone in love with status, or seduced by power, and his unassuming manner was refreshing. But he nevertheless had his struggles with humility.

Because of his own background and his years as abbot, there was that element within his temperament which tended towards the expectation that his wishes would prevail. Although he was a skilled chairman of the Bishops' Conference, he could, on occasions, attempt to steamroller the meeting in the direction he wanted it to go. Nor was he above flashes of public irritation when things did not go his way. But when that happened he was usually very contrite afterwards.

I remember a rueful admission of how deeply he had *inhaled* a newspaper article which had extolled his humility. Like the rest of us he had his vanities. He was pleased when others spoke well of him, though he was acutely aware of the dangers of praise. When he said 'I don't know what hurts me more, praise or criticism,' he was expressing himself with complete honesty. He was conscious of the gap between what others might judge him to be, and what he knew about himself. He had a lifelong fear of being 'over-assessed'.

During my six years as his private secretary there would have been very few addresses or homilies at which I was not present. There was not a single occasion when I did not gain something really nourishing from his words. I told him this one day and he was genuinely taken aback, even asking whether I was pulling his leg. He possessed the special gift of *inhabiting* the words he spoke, to the extent that even the simplest and seemingly most ordinary of his reflections exerted a compelling power.

In similar fashion, his *presence* within a gathering often conveyed a sense of peace and serenity – despite the fact that he could at the same time be inwardly agitated because of some preoccupying problem. This was a vivid reminder that the sense of peace he conveyed was God's doing, a gift granted to him at a level of his being beyond his own fashioning. But it was also true that throughout his life he had prepared himself to receive that gift by persevering courageously in prayer and steadfast faith. We now know that such faith was lived out amid considerable periods of inner darkness and no little physical suffering.

Throughout the whole of Cardinal Hume's time at Westminster, the seven last words of Jesus from the Cross meant a great deal to him. He often used them as a source of his public reflections. In later years he returned repeatedly to the prayer of the repentant thief upon the cross, 'Lord, remember me when you come into your kingdom' (Lk. 23.42). This helps to explain the reason for his choice of St Luke's account of the story of the Pharisee and the publican as the Gospel for his funeral Mass. How much he identified with that tax collector at the back of the temple: 'standing some distance away, not daring even to raise his eyes to heaven, he beat his breast and said, "God be merciful to me a sinner" '.

No account of Cardinal Hume's Westminster years could be accurate without some mention of the part which the daily reading of the scriptures, and especially the psalms, played in his spiritual journey.

As a Benedictine monk, his prayer life within the ministry would have centred for many years around the psalms. Each day, the greatest chunk of the several hours he would have spent singing in choir would have focused upon the psalms; those 150 poems composed over the thousand-year period in the history of Israel which preceded the birth of Christ. The psalms have been described as a series of shouts: shouts of love, shouts of distress, of darkness and of acute suffering; shouts of faith and hope and joy; shouts of sorrow and repentance; cries in praise of God, cries of longing for God. They express the full range of human religious experience before God. For the Christian, the psalms find the fullness of their meaning in Christ.

During his years at Ampleforth that daily immersion in the psalms exerted a compelling influence upon Basil Hume's spirituality. The years at Westminster were the period when he drew heavily upon that rich investment – above all, perhaps, during those final years. He certainly had his favourites and his copy of the Psalter is heavily annotated, focusing particularly on three different groupings: psalms of repentance (Psalms 31, 37 and 50), psalms of longing for God (Psalms 41, 62 and 83) and psalms in praise of God (Psalms 146–9). The daily communal prayer life of the community at Ampleforth fashioned itself around those three elements: repentance, longing for God and praise of God. At the heart of their communal prayer was the Psalter: the prayer book of the Church, par excellence, and thus the prayer book of the monk.

In the scriptures more generally there were two texts within the four Gospels to which Cardinal Hume returned repeatedly. One was from the Gospel of St Matthew where

Jesus says to those who criticized him for eating with tax collectors and sinners 'It is not the healthy who need the doctor, but the sick. Go and learn the meaning of the words, what I want is mercy, not sacrifice, and indeed I did not come to call the virtuous but sinners' (Mt. 9.12–13). All his life long, Cardinal Hume had a profound sense of his own human frailty; of his own need for God's forgiveness. The pastoral spin-off from such an acute awareness of his own fallibility was his immense compassion for those who were there *in the ditch* alongside him. Whenever he defended *hard* teachings of the Church in public, he resolutely avoided passing stern judgement on those who might have transgressed those teachings.

The Gospel passage he came to love more than any other, and upon which he preached constantly, was Chapter 15 of St Luke; those three stories of the *lost* sheep, the *lost* coin and the *lost* ('Prodigal') son. Each of those stories meant so much to him on his own personal journey of faith that he was able to expound them with compelling authority. Above all he prized Verse 20 in Chapter 15. He referred to it as: 'the most golden verse in the whole of scripture': 'While he was still a long way off his father saw him and was moved with pity. He ran to the boy, clasped him in his arms and kissed him tenderly'.

For Cardinal Hume, this was the image of God which triumphed in his middle and later years. He had now broken away from a more demanding image of God which had, to some extent, coloured the years of his earlier development. The story of the small boy tempted by the apples in the larder is told elsewhere in this book. It is a good illustration of the movement within the Cardinal's own inner journey. The God who would say 'Take two apples!' is the God whom Jesus describes in his three parables of God's merciful love in Chapter 15 of St Luke.

Cardinal Hume was a great admirer of St Thérèse of

Lisieux and prized immensely the opportunity he was given to visit her cell in the monastery at Lisieux. One incident in particular left a deep impression upon him. The prioress pointed out to him some words that Thérèse had gouged out with a nail above the lintel of her cell: '*Jesus est mon unique amour*' (Jesus is my only love). It was an act of naked faith during what must have been a time of terrible inner darkness. In the periods of darkness which Cardinal Hume experienced down the years, the young Carmelite saint was a much valued companion and friend.

An earlier custom to which he returned with profit at a later stage in his time at Westminster was that of writing out his prayer thoughts during early mornings in the chapel. He found that the act of writing down his 'conversations' with the Lord helped not only to keep him more focused during the prayer itself, but provided a kind of 'memory bank' to which he could return at different moments during the day. Those handwritten notes were only for his own private use and he used to destroy them afterwards.

In his writing and public speaking on the life of prayer he particularly loved to dwell upon the words *desire* and *awareness*. He would take the opening verses of Psalm 41 as his introduction: 'Like the deer that yearns for running streams, so my soul is yearning for you, my God. My soul is thirsting for God, the God of my life; when can I enter and see the face of God'. He would quote some words which had touched him deeply: 'At the heart of every man, woman and child is a God-shaped emptiness which nothing else in heaven or on earth can fill because that emptiness is God-shaped'.

I was the recipient of his final teaching on prayer as he lay dying in the Hospital of St John & St Elizabeth in June 1999. It was an intensely moving experience. As I sat at his bedside, he spoke of his new realization that the whole essence of prayer was contained in the words of the Lord's own prayer. Sentence by sentence he prayed the words of the Our Father, giving a little commentary on each different movement within it. It was quite wonderful to be there, hearing for the last time this good and holy man speaking of what lay closest to his heart. It was in a real sense his last will and testament.

Ten days later, Westminster Cathedral was filled to overflowing for his funeral Mass, with millions more watching on television. No one who was present on that solemn occasion can ever forget the atmosphere of calm and peace which pervaded the whole building. There was, of course, a deep sense of aching sadness, but the overriding emotion that morning was undoubtedly one of thanksgiving for the gift that he had been. There was a sense, too, of a truly satisfying completion to a life well lived. The Cardinal had spoken often of death as the moment of ecstasy when, for the first time, we meet God face to face in the Beatific Vision. Throughout his life he had faithfully sought that *face* of God, and now his journey was safely ended. That is why the sadness of all those who loved him was as nothing compared with our happiness for him in his new future with God. As we left Westminster Cathedral after the funeral Mass, the final sentence of the homily may have been in many minds and hearts: 'If such were the gift, [Cardinal Hume] what must God be like, the Giver of that gift?'

PART THREE

Influence of a Monk-Cardinal

12

Cardinal Hume's Impact on Others

William Charles

Cardinal Hume was clearly an influential religious figure in Great Britain, Europe and even further afield towards the end of the twentieth century. The secular press, for example, took great note of what he had to say and often turned to him, the leader of the Catholic Church in England and Wales, to hear the 'voice of religion' in the country.

Some people, however, might question just how influential the Cardinal was, and perhaps point to the decline in both Mass attendance in Catholic churches and vocations to the priesthood during his time as archbishop and the ever-increasingly materialist society, which, towards the end of the 1990s, was rushing headlong to celebrate the entry into the twenty-first century with as many fireworks and parties as possible, gathered not under the sign of a Cross but under a Dome. Cardinal Hume would doubtless have worried that his influence had not always been positive and would have felt responsible for the fewer numbers going to church and the fact that vocations to the priesthood were much lower than they had been in previous years. Debate on such matters could go on for many pages. What is beyond debate, beyond doubt, is the huge impact the Cardinal made on both the religious landscape and individuals within these shores and beyond.

That impact is revealed by the countless snippets and stories that came to light when the Cardinal died: from the formal tributes of great leaders to the reverential, appreciative comments of those from whom he bought *The Big Issue*: he had made a difference to their lives.

In the broader religious framework, Cardinal Hume had strived to make ecumenism work. While this might seem hardly worthy of mention today, it is perhaps significant to bear in mind that the first Anglican service he ever attended was his father's funeral in Newcastle upon Tyne in 1960, and, of course, in those pre-Second Vatican Council days he would not have joined in the 'Our Father'. Just over 20 years later, the Cardinal, along with Cardinal Gray, Archbishop of St Andrews and Edinburgh, on behalf of all the bishops of England, Wales and Scotland, would be inviting Pope John Paul II to Britain, the first ever visit by a Pope to British soil. In the course of that visit the Pope and the Archbishop of Canterbury celebrated a special service in Canterbury Cathedral and one result of this was to continue the improvement in relations between the Catholic Church and other Christian Churches in Britain. A monumental stage was reached in 1987, at the Inter-Church Conference at Swanwick, when Cardinal Hume announced:

> I hope that our Roman Catholic delegates ... will recommend to members of our Church that we move now quite deliberately from a situation of cooperation to one of commitment to each other. Christian unity is a gift from God and in these last few days I have felt He has been giving us this gift in abundance.

The ecumenical situation was transformed.

Although even to this day not everything is plain sailing in the world of ecumenism, Cardinal Hume had made a dramatic impact. It is not within the scope of this book to delve into and argue about the theological issues still to be resolved, but rather to indicate the highlights that, in many cases, were due to the person and nature of Cardinal Hume. A special moment for him, and for many others, came in 1995 when Her Majesty the Queen became the first reigning monarch to attend a Roman Catholic service for several centuries. Queen Elizabeth II went to Westminster Cathedral for the evening service of Vespers and Cardinal Hume's own pleasure at this event was doubtless increased by the warm regard and great respect he had for the Queen. He was very touched to receive the Order of Merit from her in his last days in recognition of his services to Britain.

An example of the effect which this improvement in relations had may be seen in the history of Preston, in the North West of England. This was a town which, like many in England, had for many years seen tensions in the relations between Protestant and Catholic Christian denominations. Preston holds a major town celebration – a 'Guild' – every 20 years. In 1972, when a Guild was duly held, the Protestant and Catholic Churches in Preston organized their own separate marches in the procession.

In 1979 the Cardinal came to Preston to preach in the main parish church of the town. Representatives of the different churches were invited to attend. A young Anglican, now a clergyman, remembers sitting next to him in the church. He recalls how deeply Father Basil prayed during the service, his being turned intently towards God. When it became time for him to preach, he took his notes for his sermon out of his biretta (a form of hat), where he kept them. After his sermon, the mood between the Churches was changed. In a sense, a wall had come down so that things were never the same again. In 1992, when the next Preston Guild took place, the Churches marched together.

While the ecumenical impact is on the large stage, Cardinal Hume's impact on many individuals at a more personal level will inevitably have been less obvious to the public; but for the individuals concerned it was clearly at times very profound. One measure of this is the letters he received.

When Father Basil's terminal illness became publicly known, he received, in the few short weeks before he died, some 5,000 letters. They came from a wide range of people and from many different corners of the world. Many referred to his books and the impact they had had on the writers. It would be impossible to cover the contents of all the letters at length but they give an insight into the impact he had already had on many people. A few examples will suffice.

The letters came from a wide range of people: Anglicans, Quakers, Methodists, Baptists and Jews. There was even a letter from the Hindu community in Mumbai.

Some spoke directly of his impact on them: 'Your sincerity and deep understanding without the slightest arrogance is the one thing through several personal sadnesses that has left me with any faith in human nature'; 'I will always be grateful to God for meeting you on the Pilgrim's Way and your giving me the courage to say "yes" to the single life'; 'I have written to you many times over the years, times of anguish, sorrow and to my shame times of anger. Your warm and loving replies were always appreciated. This time I write to tell you that you are very much in my thoughts and prayers'.

But aside from the personal stories, this book tells two stories which are markedly different. They come from Europe and from Chile and tell, in their own distinct way, how the Cardinal made a difference to two vastly different groups, in two very different spheres: the officialdom of Church bureaucracy within Europe's Bishops' Conferences and the mountains of Chile, a country and a place he had never visited and yet inspired. These stories are related in the next two chapters.

13

Cardinal Hume's Influence in Europe

Bishop Ivo Fürer with
Introduction by William Charles

INTRODUCTION

When I was in Italy a few years ago I met a young Benedictine monk and got into conversation with him. It emerged that the book then being read at mealtimes in the refectory in his monastery was Cardinal Basil Hume's *Searching for God*, a book first published more than 30 years ago in 1977. This was the first time I realized that my uncle's influence in Europe was greater than I had imagined.

But Cardinal Hume's influence was not just in the written word. Three years after he became Archbishop of Westminster, he was elected president of the Council of European Bishops' Conferences (*Consilium Conferentiarum Episcoporum Europae*, CCEE), a post he held until 1986. The CCEE was established in 1971 and brought together representatives of the various Roman Catholic bishops' conferences in Europe with the aim of promoting and safeguarding the welfare of the Catholic Church.

Perhaps like similar bodies in the secular world, the work

of the CCEE is not headline-making. And yet quietly behind the scenes the voice of the Church is heard. The work of these international bodies is inevitably slow, with initiatives often taking years to bear fruit, but during Cardinal Hume's presidency the CCEE made progress in a number of areas, including efforts to improve relations between the Christian Churches in Europe.

Cardinal Martini (Archbishop of Milan 1979–2002), who succeeded Cardinal Hume as president of the CCEE said:

> What I admired most about his presidency was his calmness, candour, straightforwardness and detachment. He was not afraid to admit to being greatly exercised by certain questions or problems. He never pressed for solutions but knew how to encourage others to shape their opinions and ideas until a virtually unanimous convergence was achieved. On occasion this prudence of his could seem excessive. But then he would suddenly counterbalance it with bold gestures and words. From this position of greater proximity, I began to admire the lucidity of his vision of the present and future of the Church, as well as his qualities of trust and constructive patience. I was also enormously impressed by his absolute impartiality, his ability never to be drawn by one side or another, and his consistent frankness and resolve in expounding his own views, while always respecting the opinions of others. Such a multi-faceted, free and spiritual personality can also seem unpredictable. It is not easy to guess in advance what he will think or say on any given subject. Usually he will express himself in a slightly new, sometimes paradoxical, way, demonstrating his ability to see the question from various points of view.
>
> (Carolyn Butler (ed.) *Basil Hume by his Friends*,
> HarperCollins, London 1999, p. 77)

The secretary of the Council at the time was a Swiss priest, Father Ivo Fürer (he became Bishop of St Gallen, Switzerland, in 1995 and retired in October 2005). In reading his account of Cardinal Hume's presidency, reproduced below, it is interesting to note a number of ways in which the earlier formative influences on Father Basil show through in his approach to the work. Thus the concept of Christ in the soul is surely to be seen behind his statement at the European Ecumenical Meeting in 1978 that 'we are filled with His Spirit'. The importance he attached to prayer is also very evident and indeed calls to mind what St Benedict says very early in the Prologue to the *Rule*: 'This, then, is the beginning of my advice: make prayer the first step in anything worthwhile that you attempt'.

In the following account, Bishop Fürer sees three particularly important strands to the Cardinal's work at the CCEE: ecumenism, evangelization and peace and justice. It is interesting, though scarcely surprising, to note the overlap with his interests in his own archdiocese at Westminster.

* * *

CARDINAL HUME AS A BISHOP IN EUROPE

Cardinal Hume had a very varied influence in Europe, where he was recognized and respected far beyond the borders of Great Britain. One way he left his mark was through the work of the CCEE, which he joined in 1977. He was elected as its second president in June 1979, succeeding Cardinal Etchegaray, Archbishop of Marseilles.

The CCEE was founded in 1971, following the Second Vatican Council, to help the work of its members, the bishops' conferences of the countries of Europe. Its principal aims are:

- to foster collegiality among bishops so that bishops, as the successors to the apostles, work together as a college for the good of the Church

- to promote communication and cooperation between bishops' conferences
- to provide a point of contact with the bishops' councils of other continents
- to work for increased ecumenical cooperation
- to support witness to the Gospel message in European society.

Bishops' conferences are represented on the CCEE by their presidents. The representatives meet annually. The CCEE also organizes a meeting of European bishops, known as a 'symposium', roughly every three years. The symposia in those years comprised about 120 participants.

In the years when Cardinal Hume was president, the CCEE focused on some major issues:

- ecumenism, to promote better relations with other Churches
- methods and opportunities for evangelization, to spread the Christian Gospel
- matters relating to peace and justice.

Cardinal Hume saw the main aim of cooperation at the European level as being to help the local bishop, above all, to broaden his horizon. The Cardinal saw the CCEE's task as involving five dialogues: within the Church, with Christian Churches, with world religions, with a world that does not know God and, above all, with God.

Ecumenism

Ever since it was founded, the CCEE has been committed to ecumenical cooperation. Its most important partner in this work is the Conference of European Churches (CEC), which comprises Anglican, Orthodox and Reformed

Churches. Since 1972, there has been a permanent joint committee with five members each from the CCEE and CEC. Since 1978, they have promoted joint European Ecumenical Meetings and, since 1989, European Ecumenical Assemblies.

The first European Ecumenical Meeting in 1978 in Chantilly, France, discussed the theme 'To be one, so that the world may believe'. Cardinal Hume gave the first talk on the theme 'We cannot follow Christ unless we are prepared for unity'. He began with the words: 'We have come together as Christians. We have gathered in Christ's name, and therefore he is in our midst. We are filled with his Spirit, which drives us, guides us and strengthens us.'

The Cardinal set the goal for our common way with the words 'diversity in unity' and 'unity in diversity'. He stressed that unity should not sacrifice diversity or vice versa. He pointed to ways along which we can walk together and discussed the visibility of the Church and the meaning of local Church and universal Church, looking at ways of growing together. Even at that time, he pointed to paths towards unity that could contribute today to the Churches growing together.

Over a year after his talk in Chantilly, Cardinal Hume became CCEE president. He had to address the challenge presented in holding a second European Ecumenical Meeting. The direction taken by the second meeting was largely inspired by Cardinal Hume. He regarded it as impossible to make progress theologically in a three- or four-day multilateral discussion between participants who often did not know each other. As he said at the beginning of his talk in Chantilly, participants need to be aware that Christ is in their midst. So a second gathering ought to be a sort of retreat, with prayer at the centre. Cardinal Hume then said:

We realize that unity is a gift of God and that we must pray for it. It is not enough to say this to others; we must lead the way in prayer. In this way a second European Ecumenical Meeting ought to show that unity is a gift of God and not some kind of self-made confederation.

Cardinal Hume was convinced that Church leaders in Europe would benefit if they had repeated opportunities for silent prayer. He pointed out that St Benedict continually sought the solitude of prayer. He was also aware that participants in this kind of gathering would experience even more painfully that there are boundaries to Eucharistic community, as it would not be possible for all to share Communion.

The second European Ecumenical Meeting took place in Løgumkloster (Denmark). In his opening address, Cardinal Hume said:

It has become fashionable to speak of prayer for unity and prayer towards unity. I believe the time has come to pray ourselves into unity. There is a great difference between merely praying for unity and praying into unity. And I think that precisely this difference is the theme of our gathering

... We come together in prayer, for only in that way can we succeed, not only in getting our own priorities right, but also in opening ourselves in wonder to the Holy Spirit. Working in the Church can easily run the risk of falling into a heresy that began in my homeland – Pelagianism.[1] It is possible that we do not have enough trust in prayer, which requires an act of faith, whose fulfilment is in so many respects becoming more difficult in an increasingly divided and secularized world.

---

[1] Pelagianism teaches that humanity has full control of its destiny.

The daily programme provided for two sessions of prayer or meditation and a communion service or Mass.

After the Løgumkloster meeting, where common prayer was the focus, a common profession of faith followed. This happened in 1984 in Riva del Garda (Italy), at the Ecumenical Meeting on 'Professing the faith together – a source of hope'. The focus was the Nicene Creed, the shared creed of Western and Eastern Christians. Cardinal Hume stressed the significance of this common act of witness. In his opening address, he remarked:

> I wonder whether the secular world – or even the majority of our fellow Christians – are really able to appreciate how remarkable these ... gatherings are, and that they surely represent an outpouring of the Holy Spirit in our days.

The most important event was the ecumenical liturgy in the cathedral in Trent. The high point was the common recitation by the participants of the Nicene Creed. At the end, the participants embraced each other in the kiss of peace, an emotional sign on the path to unity. Cardinal Hume gave the concluding address. He noted:

> Our common witness would still have been an impossible dream just one generation ago. Today we ourselves can see how the Holy Spirit is inspiring Christians to work for unity and has brought us here together for a common act of witness.

The ecumenical liturgy in the cathedral in Trent brought to mind the council which took place four hundred years earlier on the same spot. The Council of Trent, which occurred at least in part as a result of the Reformation, is often presented as a council of the counter-Reformation. Therefore it was not easy, particularly for the Reformation Churches, to profess faith together where the council had taken place. Cardinal Hume alluded to this in his conclusion:

> We bishops of the Council of European Bishops' Conferences thank our brothers and sisters from the Orthodox, Reformed and Anglican Churches most sincerely for the generous spirit in which they have come to Trent today. They certainly understand that what happened here 400 years ago is still enormously important and significant for us Catholic bishops. The Council of Trent is not an obstacle to unity; rather, it points out truths that in our days are becoming increasingly part of our common dialogue.

Evangelization in Europe

The CCEE considered the spreading of the Gospel principally at the European bishops' symposia. In 1979 Pope John Paul II said, in a homily during the symposium on 'Youth and faith': 'Dealing with the question of evangelization with regard to the Continent of Europe is very weighty and of fundamental significance.'

This challenge came precisely when Cardinal Hume was elected president and he willingly accepted it. In March 1980, at the first presidential committee meeting under his leadership, he suggested that the next symposium should first define what it means to be a European. Then there should be reflection on the Gospel, on faith today and tomorrow in Europe and also on social responsibility. These considerations ought to build on the Church's work thus far. The theme chosen was: 'The collegial responsibility of Europe's bishops and bishops' conferences in evangelizing the Continent'. The 1981 CCEE meeting dealt with this theme in some detail.

Cardinal Hume pursued the issue of evangelization in the opening address at the 1982 symposium. He began by observing that this symposium was the most important to

date and asked the basic question: 'What does evangelization mean?' He found the answer – a clear proclamation
that in Jesus Christ salvation is offered to all – in Pope Paul's
encyclical *Evangelii Nuntiandi*. He discussed what it means to
speak of Europe as 'mission territory'. He pointed out that
national bishops' conferences have an important role to play
in evangelization and concluded by identifying the obstacles
to evangelization in Europe: the lack of unity among
Christians, threats to peace and secularism. In the discussion a broad range of opinions were expressed. Towards the
end of the symposium, it became clear that it would not be
possible to produce a common text. In view of the enormous
variety of suggestions, all the participants were grateful that
Cardinal Hume, a former abbot, led the assembly with
consummate skill. The bishops present realized that more
work was necessary.

After this, there were further developments. On the basis
of the work done in the symposium, bishops' conferences
were asked what were the most important and urgent
questions regarding the evangelization of Europe. The
responses were compiled in time for the 1984 meeting. The
CCEE leadership recognized that secularization was of
great significance. The 1985 symposium was therefore
devoted to 'Secularization and evangelization in Europe
today'. Preparatory materials were made available before
the symposium. These were discussed in regional preparatory meetings, to help analysis and to identify what had
changed before an evaluation was made. This analysis
needed to continue during the symposium before there
could be a successful evaluation of the theme of evangelization.

In the opening address, Cardinal Hume pointed out the
importance of a profound analysis. Most of our contemporaries would see the changes in Europe as signs of decline and
breakdown. There was an element of truth in this, but he

143

noted immediately that the changes also offered positive signs of new life and fresh growth. In evangelization, attention should be given to this, above all. Evangelizers ought to be on their guard against an attitude of moral superiority and judgment of the world: 'The [Vatican] Council helped the Church to set aside an attitude to the world of disapproval and contempt in favour of an approach characterized by openness and insight, one which recognizes the signs of the times.'

Cardinal Hume's closing words were particularly significant. He summarized the very varied considerations and suggestions that had been made and could be helpful for further work in dioceses. He concluded with personal reflections central to which was his view that the Church is a community in the Holy Spirit:

> It must be a community that speaks to others and listens to them, a community where everyone has his or her own responsibility and can rely upon others for help; a community that can suffer with and at the same time support, that helps and takes care of whoever is in need. In other words: dialogue, co-responsibility and *diakonia* [work for a just distribution of our common resources].

He pointed out that there needed to be a greater sharing of responsibility at all levels of Church life and its missionary task. In his detailed comments he began not 'above' but at the level of parish communities, deaneries and the local Church, before moving on to cooperation between neighbouring dioceses, bishops' conferences, CCEE and the universal Church. Evangelizing today takes place in a fourfold dialogue, he said:

> First of all, there ought to be a real dialogue in the Church itself, carried out with mutual respect. Then there ought to be a stronger and more trusting exchange between Christian

Churches, so that we may become what we became in baptism – one body and one spirit in Christ. Thirdly, in a world that has broadened our horizons through the steep increase in travel possibilities and has brought other peoples closer to us, we should speak with the other world religions in order to discover what God is saying in them, and, for our part, to offer the truth we live. Fourthly, we must enter into a dialogue with the whole of society. The Church must be wherever people are and be actively involved. Worldly wisdom, too, can teach us particular aspects of the truth about God. Then, on our part, we can point to the transcendent and infinite that lies behind whatever is partially true and transient.

In March 1987 Cardinal Hume stepped down as president and Cardinal Martini, Archbishop of Milan, took his place. But Cardinal Hume continued to make his experiences and insights available to the CCEE.

In 1989/90 communism collapsed in Eastern Europe – the great turning point for the Continent. In a letter in 1989, Cardinal Hume suggested discussing European unity in greater depth at a Church meeting in 1992. This led to a proposal for a European Catholic gathering or an enlarged symposium involving 200 bishops. At the same time it became clear that the European Forum of National Lay Associations, the Council of European Priests' Conferences and the Union of European Major Superiors' Councils were working on a similar theme. In a discussion between the CCEE president, Cardinal Martini, Cardinal Hume and myself as secretary general, it was suggested an enlarged symposium should be prepared, and meet in Prague. Cardinal Hume agreed to lead a working group to prepare such an enlarged symposium. A first meeting took place in April 1990 in St Gallen, Switzerland.

In January 1990, Pope John Paul II made it known that he wanted to convene a special synod for Europe. The

CCEE president, Cardinal Martini, had not been consulted and was very surprised. Because of the synod, the CCEE project was postponed. The synod ended in December 1991 and the working group for the enlarged symposium took up again at a meeting in spring 1992. Everyone was clear that the results of the synod ought to be taken into consideration. Given that the synod had above all celebrated the discovery of freedom, the symposium ought therefore to be future-oriented. The special synod had focused on experiences *within* the Church; the symposium ought therefore to turn its attention *outwards*. Its special feature was that, while it was a symposium for bishops, a substantial number of priests, religious and lay people would also take part. Cardinal Hume attached great importance to this joint element. It was also noted that, in the Bishops' synod, people had often spoken very negatively of the West. Therefore, the coming symposium ought to see both the positive and the negative and, above all, refrain from abstract ideologies.

The enlarged symposium took place in September 1993 in Prague on the theme 'Living the Gospel in freedom and solidarity', with 100 bishops, 50 priests, 50 religious and 70 lay people in attendance. Cardinal Hume gave the introductory talk, entitled 'Reflections on the future of the Church in Europe'. He started by describing the situation that had arisen after the great change in Western and communist countries. He referred to the experiences of the special synod and took great pains to give a fair evaluation of developments in both parts of Europe. He shed light on the concepts of 'freedom' and 'solidarity' and spoke of communism's legacy and of freedom and solidarity in the West. He asked what the Church's task in Europe today could be, in a context of the themes of freedom and solidarity, and set out a personal list of practical tasks.

The first task to which he referred was prayer and witness. He saw the importance of the task of contemplative orders as a reminder of and a way towards a life of loving intimacy with God. He went on to point out the particular witness of martyrs, and mentioned participants at the symposium who had suffered under communist regimes.

The second task was to advocate justice and work for peace. The Cardinal mentioned the need to pursue these in discussing the following issues: the implications of economic development; unemployment; the responsibility of the West to post-communist peoples and also towards the Third World. In this context, he focused on the problem of migrant workers and the flood of refugees, noted the rekindling of nationalism and how the Church needed to help people to live not only in solidarity with their own nation but, more importantly, also in solidarity with humanity as a whole. He recognized that, although the end of the Cold War had reduced the danger of war, the promotion of peace is far more demanding than the prevention of war through deterrence.

The third task was the promotion of Christian unity, especially in Europe, the continent of divisions. At the same time he pointed out how important the relationships with Judaism, Islam and other world religions were in the changed situation in Europe.

The fourth task he mentioned was the role of the laity. He recognized with gratitude a growing awareness of the participatory role of the laity and a willingness for them to take responsibility in the Church. Here he made special mention, too, of the role of women.

He saw the Church's fifth task as her promotion of the family.

In these comments, one can see how much he had absorbed the lessons of the symposia on evangelization and ecumenical cooperation, and, in particular, those of the European Ecumenical Assembly.

Cardinal Hume remained faithful to the CCEE. In the 1996 symposium on 'Religion as a private thing and a public matter' he gave the homily. In it he noted that, in Eastern Europe, communism had sought openly to eliminate religion, but that the same was happening in the West, although with subtler methods. He said: 'We should never allow religion to be relegated to the edge of society. What the Church has to offer society is nothing less than the truth about man, revealed in its fullness in Christ.'

Working for peace

'Peace in Europe' was always an important CCEE theme. The main emphases were on common declarations, mainly in cooperation with the CEC, to express shared Christian views on the need for peace. Already at the first European Ecumenical Meeting in Chantilly in 1978, peace was the focus of attention, together with unity of the Churches. There were two talks on this subject. The *Declaration of the European Bishops' Conferences on the Responsibility of Christians for Europe Today and Tomorrow* (1980) argued the need for a more human Europe, for human rights and also for peace.

A problem for the CCEE was that, in communist states, the term 'peace' had been misused in order to create divisions in the Catholic Church. The *Pacem in Terris* movement in the former Czechoslovakia (a pro-communist regime organization which some clergy joined) was one example of this, as was the Berlin Peace Conference, which was rejected by the bishops in the German Democratic Republic (the former East Germany).

When Cardinal Hume was president he had to deal with sensitive political issues which are to be seen in this context. At the beginning of the 1980s, a CCEE/CEC joint committee meeting was due to take place in Moscow. Shortly beforehand, Cardinal Hume made some remarks about nuclear armament. He was unable to take part in the CCEE/CEC meeting, given the danger that the Soviets would politically misuse the fact that he was taking part. Other members of the joint committee also had doubts. In the end the meeting was postponed since 'several participants found themselves unable to take part'.

In July 1981, Patriarch Pimen wrote to Cardinal Hume and me, to tell us that representatives of all Churches and religions in the USSR had gathered on 1 July and had expressed the desire for a gathering of the heads of all the world's religions. On 12 July, the then Metropolitan (later Patriarch) Alexei visited me. He wanted to encourage Cardinal Hume to take part in a preparatory committee for a conference on disarmament in Europe. In September, the Cardinal replied that, because of prior commitments, he would find it impossible to take part in the preparatory meeting in October. He pointed out that the CCEE meeting would consider the patriarch's appeal and also that as a worldwide initiative it was within the competence of the Holy See, rather than the CCEE.

The 1981 CCEE meeting discussed the theme of peace. There was a discussion about whether a common document of the European bishops on peace ought to be elaborated as a continuation of the 1980 declaration on Europe. Cardinal Hume spoke very much in favour of delivering a message of hope.

The 1983 meeting once again discussed issuing a declaration on the common responsibility for peace. Bishops' conferences sent in various statements on peace and the CCEE asked the secretaries of the bishops' conferences to express their opinions before the meeting. A draft text was composed. This draft was discussed and voted on at the March 1987 meeting of the presidents of bishops' conferences. The presidents each signed this message, which discussed:

- the Gospel message of freedom
- the need for reconciliation among Christians
- Europe's history of wars and reconciliation
- the great task: building trust; promoting peace through the power of the truth; the Church's contribution to the promotion of peace.

This declaration was agreed on Cardinal Hume's last day as president.

Cooperation among Europe's bishops

As Archbishop of Westminster, Cardinal Hume was deeply concerned with the question: 'What do the Second Vatican Council statements on collegiality mean for an individual bishop?' As CCEE president, he was faced with the question: 'What does collegiality mean for bishops in Europe?' He expressed his concern about this in his opening address at the 1979 meeting. He stressed that a bishop's first duty is to lead the diocese, the local Church. He quoted the *Dogmatic Constitution on the Church* on the task of the local bishop:

> This power, which they exercise personally in the name of Christ, is proper, ordinary and immediate, although its exercise is ultimately controlled by the supreme authority of the Church and can be confined within certain limits, should the usefulness of the Church and the faithful require that.
>
> (*Lumen Gentium*, 27)

A change in the way meetings were held showed that collegiality among bishops benefits from human closeness. The 1979 meeting took place in the Palazzo San Carlo in the Vatican, and each bishop lived in his country's Roman college. This changed during Cardinal Hume's presidency:

the representatives of the bishops' conferences agreed to live, pray, get to know each other better and hold their working sessions in the same house. At first this took place near Rome, but later it went a step further. Since 1983, the CCEE has met in different European countries.

Zagreb, in what was then Communist Yugoslavia, was chosen as the meeting place for 1983. A Mass was concelebrated by bishops from the whole of Europe, at the end of a Eucharistic Congress with more than 10,000 participants. It offered support to the Yugoslavian bishops' conference and to the faithful. Western bishops experienced at first hand their brothers' situation in a communist country. At the conference's opening, Cardinal Hume pointed to the significance of Christian culture and action, which were threatened by philosophies and ideologies hostile or alien to Christianity. He wondered what it might mean to be involved in mission against this backdrop in this traditionally Catholic part of Yugoslavia, dominated by communism.

Cardinal Hume's great desire was that, in addition to the bishops who took part, the bishops' conferences should take up the symposiums' recommendations. He was convinced this would be encouraged if the Pope were to take an active part. This request was discussed with the Pope in 1982. Cardinal Hume's wish was that the bishops concelebrate with the Pope, and that the Pope give an address taking up the conclusions of the symposium. Might it be possible for the Pope to take an active part in the symposium? Could he not, as a bishop, have a discussion with his fellow bishops, as a member of the College of Bishops, without his contributions being invested with definitive papal authority? The Pope received these suggestions with great interest, but said he needed to consider whether this might set a precedent that he would be unable to honour at the assemblies of other continental councils of bishops. The suggestion came to nothing; the time was not yet ripe.

In a discussion the presidential committee had with the Pope in 1983, Cardinal Hume once more took up the theme of cooperation at a European level. He asked the Pope if he could convene a special synod for Europe. The Pope answered that he had not thought of this before, but that he would be prepared, in principle, to convene one. He immediately made the point, however, that its preparation would be a matter not for the CCEE but for the Synod Secretariat, the Vatican body responsible for convening Synods. The CCEE presidential committee would have been happier if the CCEE had been responsible for preparation, but as it turned out the special synod, as already mentioned, met in late 1991. Cardinal Hume regretted that the CCEE was not involved in the preparation of this synod.

During this discussion with the Pope, Cardinal Hume stressed that it was very important for the *presidents* of bishops' conferences to take part in the symposia, because effective cooperation in Europe would depend on their involvement. He wished that, whenever possible, bishops' conferences should elect their presidents as their delegates to the CCEE. At the end of his time in office he presided over the first meeting of the presidents of Europe's bishops' conferences in March 1987 near Frankfurt. In his opening address he stressed that this first meeting was a historic occasion. The suggestion that there should be an annual meeting of the presidents of Europe's bishops' conferences was accepted unanimously. In accordance with the Pope's wishes, the CCEE's 1995 statutes provide that bishops' conferences should be represented by their presidents. Cardinal Hume's request was finally adopted after more than a decade.

Cardinal Hume sought to persuade the Pope to express his support for the CCEE after the synod of bishops in 1985. In a letter in October of that year, he asked the Pope to write to the bishops of Europe in support of the CCEE's work. In his letter he made several suggestions about the possible content of such a letter from the Pope. In January 1986, Pope John Paul II wrote to the presidents of Europe's bishops' conferences, praising the CCEE's work and advising them to cooperate more broadly and more intensively.

*

The CCEE also cultivated permanent contacts with the European organizations of priests' councils, lay people and religious. It offered its members opportunities to pool experiences and cooperate in the areas of religious teaching, migration, tourism, communication and media, peace and human rights, pilgrimages, pastoral care for young people and ecclesial vocations. An important task for the CCEE in the period Cardinal Hume was president was fostering contacts between bishops' conferences in Western Europe and those in the communist zone.

*

Cardinal Hume led the union of European bishops as a confident diocesan bishop and at the same time as a Benedictine who always weighed up whether a journey was really necessary and useful. He contributed a great deal to the realization of collegial responsibility and cooperation between Europe's bishops and to an awareness of the shared responsibility of priests and religious and lay men and women. At the same time, he recognized that full realization of collegiality, in the sense of the Second Vatican Council, would require further work. He developed ecumenical cooperation in Europe and gave generously of his deep faith and his Benedictine spirituality. His vision of the Church's work was far in advance of the understanding of many of his contemporaries. Much that he said and lived is just as relevant now as it was then for the Church on her path towards the future.

14

Inspiration for a Lay Movement in Chile

Jonathan Perry and Gigi Blumer

One interesting story about Cardinal Hume's influence comes from South America where a lay Catholic movement in Chile known as the Manquehue Apostolic Movement today regards the Cardinal as a deep inspiration. *Manquehue* – the word means 'place of the condor' – is the name of a mountain on the outskirts of Chile's capital Santiago where Manquehue began in the 1970s. Today it runs three large schools, a hostel for homeless women, a community and retreat centre in Patagonia and has over 1,500 men and women taking part in weekly groups for shared *lectio divina*.

There, in that long thin land that runs 3,000 miles down the Pacific coast, from the Atacama Desert to Cape Horn, hemmed in between the Andes and the sea, the wisdom and teachings of a most English of Catholic churchmen has found fertile soil and has produced abundant fruit.

AN UNLIKELY STORY

The impact on a founder

It all started in the early 1980s when Manquehue's founder,

José Manuel Eguiguren, took a plane to England in search of some guidance in the difficult task of setting up the new movement he had begun a few years before. He had a lot on his mind as his wife had just had their first child. The young movement was looking to start a new school and they wanted it to be a Benedictine one. José Manuel was already very close to the monastery of Santisima Trinidad in Las Condes, but as it was a contemplative community without an apostolate in education, he found he needed to look further afield. A monk at the monastery in Santiago advised him to go to Ampleforth, where he was sure that the then headmaster, Father Dominic Milroy, whose mother had been Chilean, was just the sort of person who could help and Ampleforth the sort of place José Manuel needed. And so it was that he found himself bound for a country he had never been to before, not knowing quite what to expect, aware that the Holy Spirit was at work, all the way to Ampleforth, perched overlooking a beautiful Yorkshire valley, with its school and monastery whose abbot until 1976 had been Basil Hume.

When José Manuel turned up in October 1981 the community was 100 strong, with a large number of parishes to look after, a house of studies at Oxford, a retreat house and a large public school to run. At the heart of all this vibrant life lay the liturgy, the constant round of the Divine Office and the celebration of the Eucharist. He wrote:

> On first arriving at Ampleforth before I even spoke to anyone, I immediately felt at home. This is what I had been looking for, a place where the human and the divine seemed to converge. Where anyone, whoever they were, seemed to have the chance of feeling at home. The monastery and school at Ampleforth were a powerful experience of God for me, and they still are today.

He went back the following year, returning again and again in subsequent years, each time accompanied by other members of Manquehue, upon whom the place had a similar effect. José Manuel noted that:

> It is difficult to put it into words: we found at Ampleforth a rich diversity of ideas and options, all held together by the strong bond of love in community. We found men who were fiercely loyal to God and their brethren, and gently tolerant of those among them who sometimes went astray; all of this founded on prayer, community life and a rich diversity of apostolate. Here was an ideal to aspire to in our apostolic movement in South America.

José Manuel was eager to absorb all he could. He devoured everything Father Dominic Milroy gave him to read about education and life in community. Father Columba Cary-Elwes taught him how the *Rule of St Benedict* can be applied in lay life. On his annual visits, Father Timothy Wright started to involve him in his house retreats and in later years Abbot Patrick Barry was to play an important role as guide and counsellor. But it was in 1982 when José Manuel bought a copy of *Searching for God*, Cardinal Hume's talks to the monastic community during his 13 years as Abbot of Ampleforth, that he discovered in print a wealth of wisdom and teaching which he could take away with him, ponder at length and share with Manquehue back in Santiago. *Searching for God* quickly became his constant companion: he would read it along with the *Rule of St Benedict*, frequently consulting and quoting it in writings and talks. Looking back on those early years he comments:

> What Abbot Basil said to his monks in the conferences that appear in *Searching for God*, and the way he said it, taught me how to apply the *Rule of St Benedict*. I found what Abbot

Basil said to his community of monks a complete inspiration. It shed light on many of my own ideas and intuitions. What I read gave me the confidence to put many of my own ideas and thoughts into practice in the day-to-day task of leading a community of lay people in Santiago. It was a revelation then as much as it is today. I still very much treasure the copy I bought in 1982 and often carry it around with me.

Sharing his wisdom with a whole community

At that time there were about 150 members in the Manquehue Apostolic Movement. They had successfully started Colegio San Benito, and a new school for the poor, Colegio San Lorenzo, was in the pipeline. Some members were getting married, while others were considering a celibate vocation, but all were lay and all young. Many of the most committed members were working full time in Colegio San Benito alongside José Manuel, who along with his many responsibilities as founder of Manquehue and headmaster, was busy bringing up his growing family. Other members were at university and worked part-time with the boys and girls of the school. A great sense of purpose abounded and there was excitement at the challenge of being at the beginning of something new.

José Manuel ordered copies of the Spanish translation of *Searching for God*, '*A la Busqueda de Dios*', and encouraged members of Manquehue to read it. He had found it difficult to transmit what Ampleforth had meant to him but Cardinal Hume's book was a way of introducing them to its spirit, in addition, of course, to the wisdom of the man himself. To his great delight what they read seemed to connect with their own experience in the same way as it had connected with his. This was an important moment. Books should not be foisted on others and José Manuel was aware of this; people cannot be *obliged* to find them meaningful and inspiring. But as they read Cardinal Hume they found that the words seemed to speak to them about things that were happening to them in their own work, prayer, community life and friendships, and resounded at the level of their deepest hopes, problems and feelings. Talks given by an English Benedictine abbot to his monks and novices in North Yorkshire were making a profound impression on a group of young lay people thousands of miles away in another country, another culture.

In his introduction to *Searching for God*, Cardinal Hume talks about the desert and the market-place:

> In the monastic world of the West there has always been a tension between the two. Is the monk a person who withdraws into the desert to pray and be alone with God, or is he someone who goes out into the market-place to mingle with and serve the people?
> (*Searching for God*, Abbey Press, Ampleforth 2002, p. 11)

This reality was the one experienced by the community at Ampleforth in the 1960s and 1970s, a time of change both in Church and society; and the words the abbot had spoken to his monks answered similar challenges that Manquehue was now trying to address in Chile. The Cardinal goes on to say in his introduction:

> The conferences assembled here reflect to some degree this tension. And it is arguable that it is not altogether an unhealthy one, for in each of us, deep down, it results from the Christian attempt to respond to the twofold command to love both God and our neighbour.
>
> (p. 11)

The huge value of these conferences is the way they invite the reader to advance in the Benedictine way, not by a series of meditations or dogmatic instruction, but by practical, down-to-earth fatherly advice with transcendence of enormous depth. They talk about suffering, prayer and obedience; the difficulties and rewards of celibacy, of teaching young people, of coping with change; they give insights into the different seasons of the liturgical year – how to live Lent and Easter, what is happening at moments of commitment like ordination and solemn profession; especially he gives countless valuable pointers on how to cope with community life, how not to lose sight of its value and purpose, how to persevere and not lose heart.

Bound up with a growing movement

Not all was plain sailing however. Chile itself was still in the throes of the political and economic upheavals which beset it in the 1970s and 1980s. Society was divided along ideological lines. The Cold War was being played out all over Latin America and military governments abounded, Chile included. The Church had taken an active part in defending human rights, yet there were divisions and tensions within the Church over these issues which the Manquehue Apostolic Movement had, of course, to contend with. There were all sorts of problems to face. Questions abounded as to the nature and future of Manquehue itself. It was still very much finding its feet, unsure of itself in some ways. Lay movements were treated with a certain amount of suspicion by Catholics in Chile, as indeed in many parts of the world at that time. As a lay movement, it had begun to adopt the *Rule of St Benedict* as its fundamental guide for running its schools and itself. This was rather unusual: a monastic *Rule* for monks being applied by laity in building community in their schools, at home in the family, in prayer groups, wherever people met to live, pray and work together.

The Manquehue Apostolic Movement continued to grow in size and commitment. New initiatives began: a third school in 1995; a hostel for homeless women in 1999; a community and retreat centre in Chilean Patagonia in 2001; dozens of new groups for shared *lectio divina*; community houses; and, perhaps most important of all, the consolidation of the Community of Oblates of Manquehue – a core group, at the heart of the movement, of men and women, married and celibate, who had made a life promise to live, work and pray together. And all along, in this process of building a living, working community, the Cardinal's wisdom and teaching could be seen to be making a vital contribution, a quiet presence but an unequivocal influence on the creative growth of a Benedictine movement in its founding phase.

Some members of Manquehue were fortunate enough to meet Cardinal Hume. José Manuel was the first: he told the Cardinal about the influence he was having in Chile. When others went, they, too, made a point of letting the Cardinal know of the way his books were so valued by members of Manquehue. Indeed, copies of *In Praise of Benedict* and, as time went on, other writings, made their way out to Chile, but it was always *Searching for God* that topped the list. Indeed, over the years, *Searching for God* became one of the 'key texts' alongside *Spiritual Friendship* (St Aelred of Rievaulx), *Reading God* and *Collaciones* (Dom Garcia Colombás OSB), *The Life of St Benedict* (St Gregory the Great) and *The Way of a Pilgrim* (anonymous) used by Manquehue in their formation programme; and yet the Cardinal always expressed a certain amount of surprise when he was told about the effect his writings were having in far-away Chile. Perhaps he was being genuinely humble, but it seemed that he found it really rather difficult to believe the tales of his being 'a hit in Chile'. It was, after all, an unlikely story. Nevertheless, he was always encouraging about Manquehue: 'Carry on with what you're doing'; 'this is what happens when the Holy Spirit is at work'; 'this is a form of religious life for the future', were comments he made when Manquehue members who visited him told him about what was going on in Chile.

UNDERSTANDING THE CARDINAL'S INFLUENCE

What was it about Cardinal Hume that made him so appealing to the members of the Manquehue Apostolic Movement back in the 1980s when José Manuel Eguiguren first encouraged people to read him? What was it that continued to make him such an influential person for members of Manquehue throughout the 1990s and, indeed, still makes them connect with his teaching and message today?

Down-to-earth guidance for community living

When asked about what makes Cardinal Hume's message so powerful, the first thing that people mention is how easy he is to understand when speaking or writing about serious spiritual matters. They say that he seems to speak to them about experiences they have had, in a down-to-earth, accessible way. This may, of course, say something about the sort of Benedictine life members of Manquehue lead (that this enables them to identify themselves with what he is talking about), but it also says a lot about Cardinal Hume. 'What strikes me most is the simplicity and humanity with which he deals with faith and spiritual life,' says one member of Manquehue. A teacher in Colegio San Benito comments on how *Searching for God* describes 'every-day living in such a simple and real way'. Other members note how the Cardinal's words made sense to the young people they worked with in Chile: 'His language is direct. He talks about real community situations. His message is both simple and profound'; 'It's his language I find so attractive: easy to understand, homely, fatherly and natural. He talks about everyday problems and gives practical, common-sense advice'. Time and time again people mention the way they feel that Cardinal Hume talks to them personally, one-to-one, whenever they read *Searching for God*. For many, just as they were for José Manuel when he first read them, the talks are a source of constant inspiration that don't lose their freshness.

Humility, weakness, tolerance and humour

One of the keys to community life is humility. In part this involves recognizing one's own limitations, but it also means tolerating the weaknesses of others. This is one of Cardinal Hume's messages that has most struck home among members of Manquehue. A young woman history under-graduate wrote:

> *Searching for God* has taught me a lot about community life. There was one particular phrase that struck me and has helped me ever since. Basil Hume, speaking to the novices, tells them that, 'And remember, if someone is getting on your nerves, you are almost certainly getting on his.' The phrase is very simple. For many it may pass by unnoticed, but for me it meant learning to tolerate, putting up with other people's weaknesses, but above all it means that I ought to take a look at my own behaviour before I judge others.

When he is speaking to his novices who are embarking upon monastic life, Abbot Hume laid particular emphasis on the conscious decision they needed to make to think twice before criticizing or dismissing customs or aspects of community life which may at first sight seem pointless: 'Ours is a well-tried manner of approach ... Be sensitive to the experience of those who are helping and guiding you.

Try to appreciate and understand before you criticize.' This predisposition to listen and to make the effort to understand can be extraordinarily difficult, but at the heart of it lies the fundamental concept that all of us are imperfect, needing to undergo a process of formation and conversion. And to do this we need to belong to a community which is bigger than us – and we need to be humble.

This predisposition to be guided has become increasingly important in Manquehue because the members have discovered in it another of the paradoxes which Abbot Basil talks about in *Searching for God*: 'Perhaps a better word than humility is freedom – internal freedom' (p. 34). If a person makes the step to admitting that his or her own opinions or preconceptions may not necessarily be the only possible ways of doing things, and learns to try to discover the wisdom underlying the guidance offered to him or her, there comes a curious freedom from the necessity constantly to prove one's point, and so it becomes possible to be:

> free to find Him who, as the *Rule* says, is the 'source of all our desires'; free to love – you cannot love unless you are free . . . That kind of freedom will be . . . the basis of your happiness, the basis of your cheerfulness.
>
> (p. 35)

This shows that the point of humility is not to spare those in charge from the inconvenience of complaints or suggestions – far from it. The point of humility is the inner transformation that is worked in the disciple, and as usual Abbot Basil is practical and down to earth when he talks about it:

> It is very, very, difficult to be humble . . . we will find situations, circumstances and persons who will impose upon us the necessity to become humble – a quality difficult to attain and yet basic, for it entails emptying ourselves to be

filled with the spirit of Christ ... Furthermore, our daily experience of inadequacy and weakness forces us, in a remarkable way, to be humble; and humility is the basis of the spiritual life ... We try to solve a problem of frustration by bending and changing circumstances, so as to remove difficulties and obstacles. But the true religious does this by changing not circumstances but himself, by refusing to allow his peace, the depth of his union with God, to be affected by what goes on around him. More than that, he comes to see that the difficulties, obstructions, which are the source of his frustrations, are not obstacles to union with God but stepping-stones to this union. He sees God working in his life.

(pp. 81, 93)

Everyone in community is 'sick' in some way. This is another idea that people have found helpful. One person wrote:

When I read Basil Hume, bit by bit, thoughts and ideas began to sink in, phrases like 'the ideal community doesn't exist' or then again, the idea that a community is 'rather like being in a hospital where the matron as well as the patients are sick. You are not entering a community of saints'. All these ideas have been enormously helpful to me.

The need for a sense of humour has been another key message taken to heart by members of the Manquehue Apostolic Movement. Cardinal Hume urges his novices not to take themselves too seriously: 'Take *life* seriously. Take *God* seriously. But don't; please don't take yourselves too seriously.' This, one Manquehue member said, 'has helped to set me free from being too inflexible and demanding. It has helped me to learn to love and given me the freedom to be able to care more for others'.

165

The centrality of prayer

Cardinal Hume has helped many people in Manquehue to pray. The centrality of prayer is one of his most forceful and constant messages. 'Pastoral work will be successful in the truest and deepest sense only if the monk is a man of prayer' is a simple statement from *Searching for God* that has been taken very seriously in Chile. The opening words of the book, about the desert and the market-place, have encouraged many people to endeavour to find quiet 'desert' times of prayer in the midst of a busy day at work, at university or with the family. The role of the Divine Office, of the need to look at one's day not so much as work punctuated by prayer, but rather prayer punctuated by work, is yet another idea that has caught the imagination of people in the Manquehue Apostolic Movement. The role of *lectio divina*, prayer understood as a search for God, as desire for God, as discovering God's love; the way human love can be experienced as a stepping-stone to God's love; the whole idea of 'the prayer of incompetence': these are just some of the concepts that men and women refer to when they speak about what they owe to Cardinal Hume. 'What on earth could a married Chilean woman with four children get out of a book written by an English cardinal to his brethren?' was a question one member asked herself when she began reading *Searching for God*. 'I found out that the answer was, an awful lot! Above all he pointed out the danger of slipping into mere activism. He encouraged me to become a woman of prayer.'

Benedictine instinct

Early on in *Searching for God*, Cardinal Hume talks about the importance of developing a 'monastic instinct':

> It is a kind of instinct by which one is able to judge what is fitting for a monk and what is not. This can cover a wide

spectrum of action, attitude, speech, the way we pass our
holidays, how we spend money, the kind of hospitality we
give, the kind we receive, our behaviour, things we say, our
values.

(pp. 23–4)

This concept has been explicitly taken up by José Manuel
Eguiguren in the guidelines he has laid down for the oblate
community. The 'oblate instinct' is a way of expressing the
need for one's vocation to permeate every word and action,
every thought and deed, and not just be a matter of the
external, visible way in which a Manquehue oblate
organizes his or her life. It is the ease with which Cardinal
Hume brings the essence of Benedictine spirituality right
into the living, breathing daily reality of his monks' lives
that has helped Manquehue to be aware of the need to
instinctively keep one's feet on the ground in order to have
one's mind focused on heaven.

Love and personal relationships

Cardinal Hume deals masterfully with the issue of personal
relationships and love in general. Indeed, in almost all his
writings he never fails to remind people that the Christian
life, community life, is a matter of learning *how to love*. In his
In Praise of Benedict he talks about a Benedictine community
being 'A school of love' and *Searching for God* certainly
reflects this vision. This has been another compelling aspect
of Cardinal Hume's teaching. 'He has taught me how
central love should be in my life,' writes one member, 'he
has taught me to be loyal and faithful in my search for love.'
Another conjectures that:

> Cardinal Hume must have been highly observant and
> deeply interested in the people he lived with and met. This
> comes through forcefully when he speaks to his monks, so

167

much so that he has made me want to get to know the people I live and work with better. He has told me in no uncertain terms to become more human. People should matter more to me. I should not be frightened of getting involved with them, of getting to know about their lives, and their needs.

Cardinal Hume's advice on how to handle friendships, affection and emotions is honest and practical. Above all it is founded on an immense trust in God's love and power and this is never more the case than when he addresses celibacy. His down-to-earth treatment of personal relationships and his simple gratitude for the graces celibacy imparts have been of untold value to those members of Manquehue who have felt called to respond to their Benedictine vocation in this way; particularly as celibacy can be more difficult for friends and family to understand in a lay context rather than in a monastic one. 'We must not then be frightened of our capacity to love.' is what he told his brethren on one occasion.

I think, however, that the art of coping with personal relationships in which one's emotions are involved is that of saying 'Yes' to others, and very often 'No' to oneself ... Celibacy must make us more human, not less, more loving, and more loveable.

(p. 58)

This and many other similar reflections have proved to be of great help and inspiration to people in Manquehue.

Authority and availability

Cardinal Hume speaks with the authority and experience of an abbot who cares for his community with skill and sincere affection. Indeed, *Searching for God* is a lesson in how to be an abbot. José Manuel is not alone in mentioning this as one of the most valuable aspects of the book. '*Searching for God* has taught me how to live in community and how to be an abbot,' comments one of the young celibate women in the Manquehue community. She goes on:

> I have had to be in charge of people in varying circumstances and Cardinal Hume has been very important for me, not just in providing me with the sort of criteria I should be applying, in encouraging me to look to the *Rule* and the Gospel, but above all by making me really want to give myself to my community. He transmits conviction about his vocation; he knows that community is a path to God. He always gives me the impression that he knows his brethren well: the sort of people they are, the stories that lie behind each one. He is under no illusions about what they are like, and yet he is courageous when he corrects them and speaks to them about the living God, regardless of whether it is the right moment or not. He gets involved in every aspect of their lives.

It is this warmth and availability mixed with the firmness of a loving father which has found an echo in a concept which lies right at the heart of the Manquehue Benedictine spirituality: *acogida*.

Acogida is an seemingly untranslatable Spanish word which essentially means reaching out to others, making oneself available in a conscious demonstration of fraternal charity. Almost every vocation in Manquehue can be traced back to a relationship of *acogida* where one member has been able to make God's love perceptible to another in the context of friendship and self-giving.

There is a rich seam of this availability present throughout much of what Cardinal Hume writes and also in what he was like towards those who met him. The Movement's members who were lucky enough to spend any time with him talk of his unmistakable Christian and Benedictine warmth, which also comes through palpably in the way he addresses himself to his monks.

Encouragement to say 'yes'

'Make your gift whole-heartedly. Make it recklessly. Love is reckless.' These were Cardinal Hume's words to a group of young monks about to make their solemn profession, words that clearly meant a lot to those he was talking to in 1966. But words like these have also spoken powerfully to members of the Manquehue Apostolic Movement in their path to making a life commitment to their Benedictine lay community in Chile. People are, of course, assailed by doubt when deciding whether to make a promise to join a community for life. Responding to a call is never easy. Yet Cardinal Hume's talks to his novices at their solemn profession have been deeply reassuring for those at the critical moment of making the step to say 'yes' for life. 'Before making my oblation his advice to his novices before their solemn profession rang deep and true', wrote one of the five English oblates who belong to the Manquehue Apostolic Movement, who continues:

> There are three questions you should put to yourself: 'Do I want to live with these persons? Do I want to do what they do? Do I see myself becoming the sort of person they are? Note how diverse we are, how different from one another'. These words were of great importance to me as they put into plain English the essence of my wanting to be part of this community, here in Chile.

A LIVING PRESENCE

Cardinal Hume died in 1999. England mourned. Moving obituaries and stories of his unique appeal abounded in the secular and religious press alike. His loss, too, was felt miles away in Chile. His writings have sunk deep into the spirituality of the Manquehue Apostolic Movement. Phrases, ideas, concepts gleaned from his books, above all from *Searching for God*, have come into common usage in retreats, conversations, lessons, writings and foundational documents. José Manuel Eguiguren further observes: 'You often hear people in the movement talk about *Searching for God*. We have absorbed his message and made his ideas our own.' In Manquehue, Cardinal Hume is a well-known name; his face is familiar and instantly recognized. Whenever Manquehue members find themselves in London, they always take the time to visit the Cardinal's tomb in Westminster; they describe how they feel at home by his tomb, how they sense his presence. In recent years young members of the Manquehue Apostolic Movement have been invited to travel to England to help out in the pastoral department in some of the English Benedictine schools. Their trip always starts with a pilgrimage to Westminster Cathedral: 'We ask for the Cardinal's intercession and when our work is over we leave it in his hands,' commented one of these young people, most of whom have read Cardinal Hume and assimilated much of his teaching. They are all too happy to be involved in the work Cardinal Hume dedicated so much of his life to: bringing God into the lives of people in the country he loved and served.

PART FOUR

Ethiopia and Auschwitz

15

Ethiopia and Auschwitz

William Charles

Much that the reader has encountered thus far in the book
has dwelt on the way prayer informed Basil Hume's work in
the world and has shown some of the influence which he had
in a wide range of places and over time. In truth, anyone
who follows the path of this man carefully will come to
realize that at times the path of cause and effect was
complex. There were instances when his work in the world
informed and nourished his prayer life and his understanding of spiritual matters. Both then inspired him to seek
to use his influence to good effect. Two stories will illustrate
this.

When in 1984 a terrible famine occurred in Ethiopia,
hundreds of thousands of people starved as bad harvests,
civil war and political intrigue deprived them of access to
food. Father Basil, as mentioned earlier, felt impelled to go
to Ethiopia. Many people asked him what he hoped to
achieve. His answer was 'It's like visiting someone in
hospital; you don't go to "do" anything there except show
concern and be with them.' The Catholic aid agency,
CAFOD, was delighted at his proposal to go as it would
heighten the awareness of a much wider audience as well as
influence governments. In going, he may also have had in

mind his own answer to the question: What is a priest? Someone who tells people that life makes sense.

Once the party had arrived in Ethiopia, it visited a number of different sites where people were starving. The situation was truly desperate. Nuns who were there to help were having to decide who to help and who was too weak to justify trying to save, that is to say who should die – an impossible situation for them. Several incidents occurred which Father Basil recalled later. One was when he was visiting a clinic:

> I was comforting a mother whose child died while I was actually in the clinic. She went away in tears and I ran to her, and got hold of somebody who spoke her language, and I put my arms round her. I could see she was Christian because she had a cross tattooed on her forehead ... I just said to her, 'I don't understand; you don't understand; but I know your little one is now in the presence of God.'

Another was when he met an old couple:

> I remember passing an old man lying on the side of the road with many others. Next to him was his wife, and they were both dying. I looked – and this was a moment I shall never forget – into the old man's eyes. We had no language to communicate but I think he guessed in some way that I was a priest and he took my hand and kissed it. I felt very, very small, because in his eyes there was a serenity, peace and human dignity which was very remarkable ... I saw the figure of Christ in him.

He also met a nun who was tending people who were disabled as well as starving. He visited her and those she was looking after and said later: 'I saw in that Sister Gabriel Our Blessed Lord ... I felt more like those starving and handicapped than like her.'

An English newspaper, the *Daily Mail,* which was following the visit recorded:

> The Cardinal patted heads and gently stroked diseased hands. He could not check the tears as a thin old man, protectively holding a shawl around his dying wife, hoarsely whispered, 'Bless you Lord. Thank you for what you do.'
>
> 'When asked to describe his initial feelings, he said: 'That's an impossible question to answer.'
>
> Holding up his crucifix, he said, 'In there lies our hope. I know that for all those poor people dying there will be life in heaven.'

One particular incident perhaps affected him more than any other. He met a little boy:

> this small boy came up to me and gripped my hand. With his other hand he pointed to his mouth. That was his way of telling me he was very hungry. I said to the interpreter: 'Tell the little boy that I've come here to go home and make certain that food is sent to him.' He went on doing this, but he also got hold of my hand and rubbed it against his cheek. I couldn't understand that, but for the whole hour I was in that camp that little boy wouldn't let go of my hand, and from time to time rubbed it on his cheek. He was very, very hungry ... I remember speaking with that boy and asking him through the interpreter: 'Why are you looking so sad?' and he answered very simply in his own language: 'I am hungry.' I could see in that face the suffering Christ, and I realized just what a terrible scourge physical hunger is. But also there was an echo from the Cross which Our Lord spoke when He said: 'I thirst', and how He thirsts for us and wants us ... Then, when the visit was ended and I had to go elsewhere, the little boy stood – I can see him now – feet astride, his hands on his waist, and looked at me almost with reproach. I could see in his face, 'Why are you leaving me behind?' I felt awful because

there was no way I could take that little boy and bring him back to England.

I realized that when you're lost and are very hungry, and you are abandoned, you have a craving for two things: for food and for drink and for love ... It was the next day when I was celebrating Mass that I understood as I've never understood before, the secret of Holy Communion. Our Lord, realizing how much we need love, how much we need to be fed by Him, had this marvellous way of doing it: by giving Himself to us.

When I visited Ethiopia ... I saw clearly how when people are abandoned and dying of hunger they crave for love and for life ... I have never forgotten that incident and to this day wonder whether that child is still alive. I remember when I boarded the helicopter he stood and looked reproachfully. An abandoned starving ten year old child ... A little boy who taught me in a wonderful way something very important about going to Holy Communion. I have often wondered since what happened to him.

Those who accompanied Father Basil commented on how well he coped with the sights he saw. A journalist who had accompanied the party on their visit, and had accompanied others, politicians and officials, as they toured the fields where the starving lay dying, said: 'That was different. He brought something to them.' I think she meant he had made them feel loved.

On his journey back from Ethiopia, Father Basil wrote a report to deliver when he returned to London. Much of it was concerned with practical measures which needed to be taken to improve the situation in Ethiopia. In addition to this, however, he also wrote out in his own hand a poem by Helder Camara which must have represented his own personal response to his time in Ethiopia.

> Am I mistaken, Lord
> Is it temptation to think

You increasingly urge me
To go forth and proclaim
The need and urgency
Of passing
From the Blessed Sacrament
To Your other presence
Just as real,
In the Eucharist of the poor?
Theologians will argue,
A thousand distinctions be advanced.
But woe to him who feeds on You
And later has no eyes to see You,
To discern You
Foraging for food among the garbage,
Being evicted every other minute,
Living in sub-human conditions
Under the sign of utter insecurity.

He later said, 'Each Christmas I find myself calling to mind my visit to Ethiopia.'

In the following years he took an increased interest in the problems of the Developing World. In the 1990s he supported efforts to reduce the burden of debts carried by developing countries, arranging a seminar involving the International Monetary Fund (IMF), senior politicians and experts to discuss the multilateral debt problem. The seminar contributed in part to the IMF deciding to work with the World Bank towards a comprehensive debt relief programme.

Two years after his visit to Ethiopia, Father Basil was asked to visit Auschwitz as the representative of the Pope, who could not go. This experience also left a profound mark on him. It was the first time he had been to Auschwitz. He described it as:

one of the most terrifying places on earth ... I stood there shocked and silent, unable to grasp the enormity of the evil done on that spot. Auschwitz remains a monument to evil, a shrine to sin ... I was sad and ashamed ... As I walked round the barracks which is now a memorial to the dead, the reality came home to me when I saw an enormous glass case occupying the whole wall of a big room and it was filled with human hair cut from corpses in Auschwitz. Much, much more had been used by the Nazis for commercial purposes. This last mound of hair remains a silent accusation. I looked and recoiled in horror ... most harrowing of all were pictures of little children lined up to be marched to the gas chambers ... You cannot go to Auschwitz and not be changed ... I could find no words to express the horror that Auschwitz represents.

There was a text framed and hanging on a wall in one of the huts. It was a quote from Hitler. It read:

I freed Germany from the stupid and degrading fallacies of conscience and morality ... We will train young people before whom the world will tremble. I want young people capable of violence, imperious, relentless and cruel.

Father Basil read this with shock. Later he often quoted it in talks and homilies when trying to inspire young people to be passionate for good and against evil.

He doubtless realized that the fact of Auschwitz's existence and history raised questions in the minds of many about the existence and nature of God. He did not react to this as some people have by concluding that either there cannot be a God or at any rate a God that loves humanity, for he later said, 'But if we ask, "Where was God in all this?" the answer has to be, "There, wherever there are human beings. In the midst of any human pain, there God suffers too".'

In 1988 Father Basil attended a service to commemorate the fiftieth anniversary of Kristallnacht, when the Nazi persecution of the Jews in Germany was significantly increased. He said, 'The memory ... must never be allowed to fade.'

Father Basil's visit to Auschwitz stimulated an increased interest in the Jewish people and their faith. He began to read *God in Search of Man* by a great Jewish writer of the twentieth century, Abraham Heschel, and found, perhaps to his surprise, that they shared a view of the nature of existence and its relationship with God. He noted that Heschel writes:

> Standing face to face with the world, we often sense a spirit which surpasses our ability to comprehend. The world is too much for us. It is crammed with marvel. The glory is not an exception but an aura that lies about all being, a spiritual setting of reality.
>
> To the religious man it is as if things stood with their backs to him, their faces turned to God, as if the glory of things consisted in their being an object of divine thought.
>
> This is one of the goals of the Jewish way of living: to experience commonplace deeds as spiritual adventures, to feel the hidden wisdom and love in all things.

Memories of Wordsworth and his lines on Tintern Abbey, read 45 years earlier, and mentioned in the chapter on his family, must have come flooding back.

Father Basil took other steps to improve his understanding of Judaism. He attended a *Seder*, or Passover meal, and found that his understanding of the Catholic Mass was almost transformed. He worked with increased vigour to improve relations between the Catholic Church and the Jewish community. One result of this was that in 1995 he attended a Jewish service to mark the fiftieth anniversary of the end of the Second World War.

When Father Basil died, the Chief Rabbi went to stand by his coffin and recited the Psalm 90, a testament to the friendship which had grown up between Catholics and Jews in the intervening years.

PART FIVE

Last Thoughts

16

Friendship

William Charles

Basil Hume was a man that many regarded with good reason as their friend, for he had an excellent memory for names and faces and took a very real and affectionate interest in many people. But as is the case with all of us, some friends were closer than others. Although he was able to mix with people from all walks of life, he felt at ease most of all with 'ordinary people' and was probably happiest sitting, drinking tea in somebody's kitchen.

There were some friends with whom he would spend some of his limited spare time on holiday. They would spend time in the countryside together, where he loved to fish and took long walks.

Father Basil kept up with old friends. He never lost touch with Cecil Foll (who died before him) or Archie Conrath, his old rugby teammates, with whom he stayed friends for over 60 years. Old memories seemed to have lingered on in ways which it is not easy fully to explain. On the occasion of one of the conclaves to elect a new Pope which took place in 1978, Father Basil went to stay with the Conraths before going to Rome. On the pillow in his room, a piece of card mysteriously appeared with the words written on it, repeating the old joke: 'Pope or Bust!'.

The Conrath parents never did find out which of their children put it there.

On another occasion, Archie was asked if he would invite Father Basil to come to a big public dinner and make a speech. Archie declined as he knew his friend would feel obliged to accept the request. A couple of years later, the organizers invited the Cardinal directly. He came and made the speech. It went very well but afterwards he asked Archie worriedly, 'How did I do? Was it all right?', the very same question he used to ask after he had finished a house 'Jaw' 30 years before.

His friendships extended to a wide variety of people and age groups. He particularly enjoyed watching sport and in what little spare time he had would often sit with younger friends to watch football (especially Newcastle United) or light, comedy dramas on television. As a friend he was honest and loyal. He could be very frank and at times severe if he thought that was best, but afterwards he would show his compassion and give reassurance. As well as being very good company, he was a great listener and totally trustworthy. Many secrets and confidences will have gone to the grave with him. This is not to say that he was always the perfect friend. He had difficulty at times in enjoying himself and sometimes could only do so if someone else took responsibility for making arrangements. He could be difficult. Sometimes he would pull out at the last minute from something which had been arranged. Perhaps it was pressure of work but perhaps also feelings of guilt at the idea of enjoyment affected him.

However, he could also be very generous. One young couple remembered an unusual act of friendship when he was Abbot:

We invited Father Basil down to our home for the christening of daughter number one and to attend

Stephanie's belated birthday party. The party went on far too long, leaving Stephanie and me in a panic about what still needed to be fixed for the christening next morning. I could not sleep properly in the early hours, but at about 4 or 5 a.m. I heard the vacuum cleaner being used and went downstairs to find the Abbot cleaning up after the party: that is true friendship.

17

Meeting Christ

William Charles

If I don't go into the desert to meet God, then I have nothing to say when I go into the market-place. That's very important.

I could only survive my work as Archbishop . . . .if I have allocated so much of the day to prayer. That has to be done, in my case, early in the morning. I don't think I could survive in my job unless I had that half hour. It has become very important to me.

Cardinal Basil Hume

Throughout his life, from the remote North Yorkshire valley to the bigger stage of Westminster and beyond, Basil Hume never lost sight of the importance of prayer and that fundamental division between the desert and the market-place which is at the heart of monastic existence. He explained once what these words meant to him. His remarks are addressed to God.

I am caught between the desert and the marketplace – in the desert there is space, solitude, silence, stillness – a sense of your presence, nothing between You and me, just You and me – as indeed is the case now in this half hour, just You and me – sometimes a Gethsemane experience, a struggle with anxieties, fears, the sense of being overwhelmed by the problems of life, or just bored or distracted – sometimes a Mt

Tabor experience[1] when we can say 'it is good Lord to be here'. I love that desert. In the market-place the world is present ... Distractions abound and temptations too. Must I flee from the market-place and go to the desert ... and yet all those people are made to Your image and likeness – drawn to them I am drawn to You, admiring them, I admire You, fond of them, I am fond of You.

For Basil Hume, the desert represented the place where he could be alone with God and pray; the market-place was the world in which he had to act in response to God's command to love others. The relationship between the two places lay at the heart of his life. He prayed to God, whom he loved above all others, and was impelled by that prayer to go out to the world, for, as he said, 'prayer leads to love'.

Many of those who met the Cardinal considered they had met a genuine man of prayer, a man of God who communicated an inner strength, a powerful and affirming sense of prayerfulness. Those who met him casually would not have guessed it, but a life of prayer was not often an easy one for him. He often described his most usual form of prayer as being 'a prayer of incompetence' and it was rare for him to experience a deeply satisfying moment of prayer. He once said to one of his private secretaries, 'I have not been successful in my prayers but I have been faithful.'

There were exceptions to his sense that his prayers had not been successful. In 1977 he recalled that in his past experience he had found that: 'twice the beatific vision caught up unexpectedly'. It is worth remembering that a truly successful moment of prayer will have a lifelong effect.

---

[1] Mount Tabor is thought to have been the mountain which Christ climbed with some of the apostles. At the top he was transformed and seen talking with the Old Testament prophets Moses and Elijah, thus revealing his true nature to his followers.

But there were also times of doubt, although he never doubted the existence of God. Principally, he did sometimes wonder whether God was loving. From what he said on other occasions it is clear his response to these doubts was to turn to prayer: 'I have often prayed ... "Lord, I do believe, help thou my unbelief".' Particular passages from the Gospel, as already mentioned, had a special importance in his heart. Several of these related to instances where Christ healed people: the story of the blind man asking to be given his sight, a deaf man seeking to have his hearing restored, a leper asking to be made clean, a lame man asking for healing. When troubled, he would put himself in the position of the blind, the deaf, the leper and the lame and ask God to help him to see, to help him hear what God wanted of him, to cleanse him of his sin and to enable him to act. He learned to treat doubt as a friend.

He encountered other problems in his spiritual life. One, he felt, was a tendency to rely on his own efforts rather than God. He said: 'Nothing in my spiritual life do I find harder than to trust ... I don't trust God enough. I do fret. I do fall into the trap of thinking that it all depends on "me".'

In addition he had feelings of personal inadequacy. When talking to some of his fellow priests he observed that:

> Deep down in every priest there is always a slight sense of unease ... we discover we are in fact too fragile to carry the hopes of those we serve ... I too have been less than adequate in my task which is to bring the good news.

As he aged, this may have become more marked, for he said:

> As we grow older we become more conscious of our failings and guilt and can very easily lose faith in ourselves ... as you grow in self-knowledge the gap between what you are and what you know you should be will become greater.

He sometimes questioned whether he deserved to hold a position of power, saying, 'I am increasingly of the opinion that no one is ever really worthy enough to exercise authority over others. As I say this, I am thinking in the first place of myself.' At times he was concerned that he had not been a good bishop, writing in a letter in 1997: 'I have been constantly anxious about the fact that I gave far too little time to our priests.' He may have been unduly harsh on himself, but he thought himself overrated.

Given his ability to identify with others and take an interest in them, we should not be surprised that he thought 'rejection, failure, fear and others such as these are the inner wounds from which we all in some measure suffer'.

Once, quite late in his life, a friend asked him if he had any regrets. After a brief pause for reflection, he answered: 'Time unspent. Love not given.' The many people who had benefited from his loving, pastoral approach to life would have disagreed.

It was probably, however, partly his willingness to be honest about his difficulties with prayer that made him a powerful speaker on the subject. For others, who also often found their prayer life hard, doubtless felt that he had experienced similar difficulties and, given his evident holiness, were encouraged to persevere. When he went on pilgrimage to Lourdes he would give one or two talks on prayer in the evenings. Fellow pilgrims were keenly interested to know, 'Is the Cardinal speaking tonight?' He was spellbinding when talking on these occasions.

If he sometimes felt a failure in his prayer life and at times in other respects, it is worth remembering that he himself considered that the test of a truly successful prayer life is whether the person concerned becomes more loving. He said:

> If you want to apply my tests as to whether your prayer is going well, then judge it according to the answers to these

questions: Am I becoming more generous? Am I growing in charity? Kinder? More considerate? More tolerant and understanding? Less self-opinionated?

He would doubtless have asked for that test to be applied to himself. The reader must judge.

In his prayer life Father Basil had a number of rules, for, as he said, 'I have to be disciplined and ordered and stick at it,' even though he accepted that 'the best way to pray is the way that suits you'. His rules were: do it, make up your mind; make space in the day for a quarter to half an hour; decide what to do the next day – like a lover waiting for the beloved, preparing what to say, thinking of a word to describe her, repeating a phrase he wants to say, just thinking about her. He recalled that 'in monastic life you were always supposed after Compline in the evening to prepare your meditation for the next day'.

Other rules were: don't look for success, don't give up; do spiritual reading, for 'the mind needs to be fed in order to stimulate prayer'; start with the New Testament and the psalms – read the Gospels as being addressed to you personally. His final rules were: give thought to what we say because through the thoughts we discover the God about whom the thoughts are; make distractions part of your prayer; plan it!

He said:

the effect of prayer is to interiorize religion, open us up to the values of another world and at the same time and profoundly, open us up to each other ... Through perseverance in prayer we are gently led to see more clearly that we are not the centre of everything but God is.

It would be wrong to give the impression, however, that his prayer life was not fruitful or that his problems were very great. On the contrary, to many of the people he met he conveyed a profound impression, a special aura. On one occasion when, as cardinal, he joined a gathering, a man said 'He has brought God into the room'.[2] A number of his comments in later years could only have been made by someone who had experienced real benefits from a life of prayer. For he said:

> One of the fruits of a life in which prayer plays a significant part is an increased longing for God ... The spiritual life of a religious does become simpler and should become deeper ... One comes to realize that the conviction which we have concerning the things of God has indeed grown stronger; that the understanding of the things of God in the experience of life are somewhat clearer.

One priest who knew him well and talked to him much in his later years says that as he grew older he developed an increasingly warm, even playful, relationship with God. The angry, frightening idea of God received in his youth had gone. It was this friend who introduced him to the idea that God's judgement involves us whispering into the ear of a loving God, more than enduring a terrifying ordeal. He took warmly to this idea and referred to it often.

The effect he had on others reflected the fruits of his years of devotion. On one occasion, a friend turned to him for help because his teenage daughter could not sleep, worrying about hell. He readily agreed to see her and she visited him twice. She recalls thinking that he was the most spiritual person she had ever met, so wise and so calm. She remembers him saying that faith is like swimming. When you take your armbands off and you push off for the first time unaided you have to have faith you will keep afloat

---

[2] From John Harriot's chapter in Tony Castle's *Basil Hume: A Portrait*, William Collins, London 1986, p. 65.

and swim. You can't prove it in advance. At some point you have to take the plunge and just believe. Her contact with him helped her enormously.

A priest recalled ringing him with a problem late at night and finding a sympathetic ear even though he had probably woken him. Later the priest had a serious operation. When he came round from the anaesthetic, who was at the bedside? Father Basil.

As far as his family were concerned he was always a rock in times of trouble and a dearly loved member of the family. He baptised many of us, conducted our marriage services and, where necessary, presided over our funerals. When my sister, cousins and I were children, he would join us on holiday every year. We looked forward to seeing him because he was such fun. On the cold Northumberland beach where we would often play he would join in with our games and was the only adult prepared to jump into the North Sea with us. Once he became archbishop it was in many ways difficult to see as much of him (and indeed we were discouraged from coming to Westminster too often, because I think he feared being seen as having 'hangers-on'). But he enjoyed it when family visited and would move the furniture so that the small boys could play football in the large rooms of Archbishop's House. He would sit happily with a small child on his knee and listen to their story. Every year he held a Christmas party for the whole family. This was a highlight of the year for the younger members, who were encouraged to play games in the large rooms and corridors of the official residence. Next door in Clergy House the noise would prompt the remark, 'The Cardinal's having his Christmas party.' He much enjoyed seeing the children set off the various Christmas musical toys that were hanging from the doors. He would then delight them by joining in and setting off as many as possible all at once, which made an appalling din.

If anyone in the family was in difficulty he was always

there to help. I know from my own experience how valuable this could be. When I was young I became seriously ill with depression, having overworked for my exams at university. I went to my uncle for advice. He assured me that if I was patient my depression would pass. It was enormously, perhaps crucially, reassuring to be told this by him, for by then he had been Abbot for over ten years and I knew that he had successfully carried great responsibilities in that job. He could be trusted to be right. I know that he helped numerous others both in the family and among his friends who had similar or other problems. We miss him very much.

One characteristic which those who knew him well loved dearly was his sense of humour. He once said, 'To be a true monk is to be a joyful one.' He certainly lived up to this ideal. His humour was kind and often pointed at himself. Not very long before he died he fell and broke his arm. He came to a family event, where my stepfather was receiving a papal award. Dressed in his cardinal's robes, he came up the stairs, his arm in plaster. He brandished his arm and said, 'You should have seen the other fellow!' Neither did his sense of humour desert him when he was dying. A few days before the end, he had a bath but was too weak afterwards to get out. The nurse took off her stockings and climbed in to help him out. She said 'I bet this is the first time you have had a girl in your bath.' Instantly he replied, 'Yes, and I bet it is the first time you have had a cardinal in yours.'

What was it about this man that made him so special to so many people? I believe that the answer is to be found in a lecture he delivered towards the end of his life in which he gave his own version of his personal story. In it he mentioned some of the events described earlier in this book: the story of the coffin, of the boy with the apples, his discovery of Wordsworth's poems, learning of love. But then he went on to speak of a meeting with Christ. This, I believe, is not to be read as a story of a literal meeting but was his way of explaining how, through people, through the Gospels, through prayer, through the *Rule of St Benedict*, at various times in his life, especially in his first years in the monastery, he had a series of experiences which he could only explain in one way: he had met Christ.

Epilogue

This book began by wondering how one person, a monk from the North of England, could have caused so much admiration in so many people. What made him the sort of person he was?

Basil Hume said the key factor in the life of a monk is that he must seek God, a lifelong task. A more eloquent testimony of Basil's journey in that task could hardly be found than that contained in the homily preached at Basil's funeral by Bishop John Crowley. The readings come from Wisdom 13.1–9, I Corinthians 1.25–31 and Luke 18.9–14.

Dear sisters, dear brothers, two short months ago when told of his terminal cancer, the Cardinal was, at first, tempted to say, 'If only ... if only I could start all over again, I would be a much better monk, a much better abbot, a much better bishop.'

'But then I thought,' – these are his own words – 'then I thought how much better if I can come before God when I die, not to say "thank you that I was such a good monk, good abbot, good bishop", but rather, "God be merciful to me a sinner". For if I come empty handed then I will be ready to receive God's gift. God be merciful to me a sinner.'

How long ago it all seems now since that famous newspaper article in September 1975. It listed for the very first time the name of Basil Hume as one of six front-runners for Westminster. Each candidate was given a little write-up noting main advantages, main disadvantages. Under the

Abbot of Ampleforth, the main disadvantage was brief and to the point. It read: 'Much too humble to make known his abilities – could easily be missed!' How grateful we are to God that he wasn't!

To his own family and some lifelong friends he was 'George' or 'Basil', to others 'Your Eminence', but to most of us he was just 'Father'. The Cardinal answered to many titles. 'How would you prefer to be addressed?' said one of his new priests way back in 1976. Back came the surprising reply – 'I can cope with just about anything short of "hey you!"'

But to all of us, whatever we called him, Cardinal Hume has been an outstanding spiritual leader, a man we shall achingly miss, and for whose life we are so grateful to God. Our first thoughts in love today are for his family, for his own personal household and staff next door (particularly the Sisters of Mercy), the priests of Westminster diocese, where he had come to feel so much at home, his monastic brethren, and his many friends. Because he was not just admired but loved, the Cardinal's death has provoked a lot of sadness, a shaking amount of personal grief all over the place.

But our main task today is to say, 'thank you, God, for giving us a shepherd after your own heart'. Isn't it already clear that, through his life, and in the manner of his dying, God has amazingly blessed us, and far beyond the boundaries of Church or religious belief?

In a quite extraordinary way it seems that everyone thought of him as a personal friend. Among the sacks full of letters which engulfed Archbishop's House when his terminal illness became known, a sizable chunk of them actually began with the words, 'I am not a member of your Church', or, 'I am not a believer'. But each letter bore its witness to a man of God who had touched people's hearts in a remarkable way. That universal appeal was somehow symbolized when Her Majesty the Queen conferred upon the Cardinal the Order of Merit. How moved he was by the graciousness of that gesture.

Now I begin to feel the Cardinal tugging impatiently at

my alb, commanding me to return to the Scriptures for this Mass, all three of which he so carefully chose. Throughout his life he was much more fearful of praise than criticism. To a friend whose virtues were being a bit over-sung in his hearing he remarked, 'Enjoy that, but don't inhale please!'

So, back to the Scriptures, and in particular to the final words of that second reading, 'As it is written, "let him who boasts boast of the Lord" '. That is surely what we want to do at this Mass. Pope John Paul perhaps can help us here. He once wrote, 'We need heralds of the Gospel who are experts in humanity, who know the depths of the human heart, who can share the joys, the hopes, the agonies, the distress of people today, but who are, at the same time, contemplatives who have fallen in love with God.'

Those words of the Pope – which incidentally the Cardinal loved and often quoted – capture well our pride in him, and our gratitude to God. For here was a monk, a bishop, who touched people's lives deep, deep down because he knew God. Because he first inhabited his words, what he then said about God rang true. It had authority behind it. He spoke to us, as someone said, from the inside out.

But here, too, was someone whose very warm human heart had been broken open, to share in God's own compassion for others, and especially for those in pain. Because his eyes were fixed on God he became vulnerable to others and especially to the poor. His very last public intervention just a fortnight ago, and virtually from his deathbed, was to support Third World countries shackled by unpayable debts. At home, too, in this country, his support for those driven to the margins of life was utterly faithful. No one who knew him had to ask the question why, why this passionate social concern? From the depth of his being he believed that every human person is made to God's image and likeness. His logic thereafter was impeccable: the less that dignity was recognized, the more he raised his voice. There was a solid earthiness about his holiness, his wholeness which was anything but other-worldly.

But here tugging at my sleeve again he would want to

strike a note of agonized caution: if a false idea of religion, as detached and purely spiritual, upset him, so too did the opposite mistake, the one made by those who would leave God out of the picture. How else to explain his provocative reading from the Book of Wisdom. Its strong meat, echoing the Cardinal's growing concern that the final judgement on our age might be: we were clever but not wise. 'If they had the power to know so much that they could investigate the world, how did they fail to find sooner the Lord of these things?'

For 35 years as monk and for 23 years as archbishop, Cardinal Hume centred himself on God. And from that store of wisdom he fed us. He addressed head-on the God-shaped emptiness which is within everyone. Without ever seeking it, he became a reassuring light for perhaps millions of people in this country and beyond. And, all the while, his deeply Benedictine soul guided him towards balance – the middle ground, the common good – but he did it without ever compromising truth; whether it be in the dialogue between Churches, between different faiths, or within his own Church.

In their two very different ways Archbishop Worlock and himself kept our Church out of the clutches of extremists, to right and left, and far away from those who, by harsh judgements, might easily crush the broken reed. Both pastors were conscious of those on the outside, of those feeling abandoned by the Church. Their Christ-like instinct was to count the stragglers in, and never out.

You will surely be glad to hear a little more about the Cardinal's last weeks in hospital. Great credit is due to the staff and chaplain at St John and St Elizabeth's, as well as to the other hospitals which had cared for him previously.

The story of those final days is of someone almost entirely at peace, preparing himself most carefully for that 'new future', as he called it, in a farewell letter to his priests.

When the doctors first told him of his advanced cancer, he went straight to the hospital chapel where he sat praying for half an hour. 'I had preached so often on the seven last words of Jesus from the Cross,' he said, 'now it was wonderful to find they were such a part of me.' All during that initial period of waiting for death he found, to his delight, that his prayer was amazingly sweet, full of consolation.

But then, to quote him, 'the curtain came down', and it was back to the darkness of faith. 'But I wasn't worried,' he said, 'because I knew what was behind that curtain.'

In those last few days here on earth he came to a fresh understanding of the Our Father. It was, he said, like discovering its inner meaning for the very first time. 'It's only now that I begin to glimpse how everything we need is contained right there in the Lord's own prayer.' In the presence of a friend he then prayed the opening three sentences of the Our Father, adding each time a tiny commentary of his own. To sit there with him and to listen to what he said was to understand afresh all that he stood for. It was to be the recipient again, in a wonderfully privileged way, of his most special gift. As few others have done he raised our minds and hearts right up into the presence of God.

He began: '"Our Father, who art in heaven, hallowed be thy name." He then paused for a moment before giving this thought: 'To sing the praises of God; it is that for which we were made, and it is that which will be, for all eternity, our greatest joy. "Thy Kingdom come": the Gospel values of Jesus – justice, love and peace – embraced throughout the whole world and in all their fullness. "Thy will be done on earth as it is in heaven": that's the only thing which really matters. What God wants for us is what is best for us.'

It was utterly marvellous to be there for that moment. In those final weeks, curtain up or curtain down, the Cardinal's one prayer was simply this: 'Father, into your hands I commend my spirit.'

Humanly speaking, it would have been so lovely to have him lead us into the millennium. It would also have been the golden jubilee of his priesthood. But that was not to be. Someone else will now break open the jubilee door into this cathedral. Someone else will celebrate the Christmas Mass which ushers in the great jubilee of Christ's birth, 2,000 years ago. He won't begrudge them that because for him now a new future beckons. All his life he had been a pilgrim, searching restlessly for glimpses of God. 'It is your face, O Lord, that I seek, Hide not your face' [Psalm 26/27].

Now that journey is over. He is safely home behind the curtain, face to face. Our deep love for him and our enormous sense of gratitude for the gift he was, provokes a final question: If such were the gift, what must God be like, the Giver of that gift?

Acknowledgements

This book would never have been produced without the assistance of many people. I am sure all will understand if I give first mention to Abbot Patrick Barry, who has been a monk since 1935. Without his encouragement this project would never have been launched. Without his contributions it would not have been possible to bring together what is here. His support has been truly irreplaceable. To write two such superb pieces as his chapters, along with an appendix for the book, at an age when most would be sitting happily on their laurels, is a magnificent achievement.

I would like also to thank a number of monks from Ampleforth Abbey who provided invaluable insight and assistance with the chapter on the early years in the monastery, which can only fairly be described as a collaborative effort. I would also like to thank the Abbot of Ampleforth for permission to publish the final chapter given to the monastic community by the then Abbot Hume in 1976.

I would like to thank profoundly Liam Kelly, whose support, encouragement and tireless advice have been of immense help and whose work on Chapter 8 was invaluable.

I must deeply thank Bishop John Crowley, who has also

been a great source of advice, encouragement and assistance in numerous ways. I am very grateful to him both for the very personal and illuminating chapter he has written and also for allowing the use of the homily he gave at my uncle's funeral in the concluding piece of the book.

I must also thank the other contributors who have written chapters: Richard Thomas for his chapter on my uncle's time as a teacher in the school, which I think shows very effectively why my uncle was so dearly loved by those who came under his charge as a schoolmaster; to Teresa de Bertodano whose chapter so vividly shows the Cardinal's continuing interest in and love for the young at a time when he was burdened with the responsibilities of high office; Sally McAllister, whose touching piece on her years at Archbishop's House adds so importantly to our knowledge; Bishop Ivo Fürer, whose fine explanation of the Cardinal's work at the Council of European Bishops' Conferences sheds so much light on a side of his life which few in Britain probably knew about; Jonathan Perry and Gigi Blumer for their fascinating chapter on his influence in Chile which may come as a surprise to the reader as much as it obviously once did to my uncle. I am deeply and eternally in debt to all of them.

Many others assisted me in my researches. These included a number of conversations with the monks of Ampleforth (principally Father Martin Haigh, Father Edmund Hatton, Father Geoffrey Lynch, Father Adrian Convery and Father Felix Stephens), and the monks of St Louis, Missouri (particularly Abbot Luke Rigby).

Some people I should give prominent mention to have since died. First are my mother and stepfather, Madeleine (née Hume) and John (Lady and Lord Hunt of Tanworth). The others are Heather Craufurd, Brendan Smith and Archie Conrath. All of them gave me hours of their time to pass on their memories. Phyllis Gibson also wrote to me with information but has since died.

I thank also Elizabeth Conrath who, too, spoke to me.

In addition, I should thank Cardinal Cormac Murphy-O'Connor for allowing me access to the Westminster Diocesan Archives and to the archivists for their assistance. My uncle's former private secretaries, Monsignor Miles, Father Gladstone Liddle, Canon Pat Browne, Monsignor Vincent Brady and Monsignor Jim Curry all gave me their time and the benefit of their advice. A number commented on drafts.

Archbishop Vincent Nichols and Father Timothy Radcliffe both gave me significant help, for which I am very grateful. I should thank also the Chief Rabbi Sir Jonathan Sacks who gave me some of his valuable time and thoughts.

My thanks also go to Father Rick Sirianni, Monsignor Vladimir Felzman, Sister Dorothy Bell, Sister Brendan Costello and Mr and Mrs Donald Cape who also passed on their thoughts and recollections

Old boys of St Bede's and other old boys of Ampleforth helped greatly by passing on their memories and insights. I should mention Bob Allison, Robin Anderson, Christopher Balfour, Paddy Brocklehurst, Mike Bufton, Michael Cain, Hugo Castelli, Leo Cavendish, Tony Chambers,William Clarence-Smith, Charles Clennell, Peter Constable Maxwell, Steven Copeman, David Corbould, Richard Defoe, Andrew Dudzinski, Frans Ellenbroek, Nick Gibson, Michael Gretton and his wife Stephanie, John Grantham, Edward Hamilton, John Horn, John James, John Jones, Bob Kelly, Stephen King, Andrew Knight, Peter Nelson, David Noton, Bart O'Brien, Hugh O'Brien, Jerome O'Brien, Richard O'Callaghan, Tony (Anthony) Osborne, Jonathan Owen, The Earl Peel, Myles Pink, Mike Sellars, Mark Shepherd, Colin Sutherland, Tony Sutton, Simon Tyrrell, Nigel Tyson, Louis van den Berg, Rupert Wilkins, Charles Young and Hugh Young. If not all have resulted in direct quotes in the text, I trust they will be assured that their contributions helped inform the background.

I received much assistance from my family. I should mention my aunts Christine Westmacott (née Hume) and Frances Kristensen (née Hume), and Pat Hume, as well as my uncle Christopher Westmacott. All have passed on their memories and read drafts where appropriate. My sister Catherine Hickman has been hugely helpful both with her own recollections but also with advice, assistance and suggestions of many kinds. My thanks also to her husband John Hickman and their children. I should thank also other members of my family including Philip and Sue Westmacott, Diana and Gerald Williams, Ragnhild and Svein Hagen and their families for their assistance and advice. I thank Dr Hewan Dewar, both for his time and for allowing me to draw on his publication, *The Story of Cardiology in Newcastle*. Other family members who helped me include Michael Gibson and his family and Vicky Bateman and her family.

Others who have helped me include Vincent Anandraj, Dr Seymour Spencer, Cathy Corcoran, Julian Filochowski, Bishop Gerry, John Gibbs, Father Deegan, Bishop Tom McMahon, Roxanna Panufnik, John Studzinski and Charles Wookey, as well as several priests of the Westminster diocese. I am very grateful to all of them. If I have omitted anyone who should be included, I apologize.

Finally I should thank my immediate family. My eldest daughter Elizabeth read drafts and gave me advice from South Korea. My second daughter Frances did the same although at university at Warwick. My youngest daughter, Mary, has been invaluable in countless different ways. Last, and most importantly, I thank my wife Christine who has been a tower of strength throughout the whole process.

In the course of my research, I uncovered a good deal of material which it has not been possible to put into what was always intended to be a short book. If at some future date someone else wishes to refer to it, it exists. There is much that remains unsaid which I am sure would interest many readers.

Although this work tells many stories about Cardinal Hume, seen through the eyes of those who knew him and worked with him, it is often his own words that complete the story. Inevitably, there are many quotations from conferences, talks, speeches and homilies that he gave throughout his life. Readers may recognize some of the texts, for, as the Cardinal himself said, all he has to say has already been published. I hope he will forgive this further publication. In working on this book, quotes have been taken largely from the original manuscripts lovingly typed by Heather Craufurd without reference to whether they may have been published or not.

Some material which is copyright to Ampleforth Abbey Trust and relates to Father Stephen Marwood and Abbot Herbert Byrne has been drawn upon from the website www.plantata.org.uk. My thanks go to the Ampleforth Abbey Trust for permission to use this.

References in the text to the Nicene Creed should be read as referring to the Nicene-Constantinopolitan Creed.

Appendix I

The Origins of Monasticism

Abbot Patrick Barry OSB

The Acts of the Apostles give an account of how the earliest Christians lived after Christ's resurrection in Jerusalem. It is a story which has haunted all who, through the ages, have sought to live a life in imitation of the highest ideals of the Gospel. The memory was cherished in the Church when it scattered and grew under the Roman Empire. When serious persecution began under the Roman emperors, a movement grew up among Christians to take refuge in the lonely places of Egypt and Syria and there live a Christian life of intense simplicity and purity. It began among hermits and developed in communities. These were the earliest monks and, when the Empire accepted Christianity as legitimate, monastic communities of the desert grew in number and strength. They were a witness against the corruptions of society but they were always an integral part of the Catholic Church in the East and in the West. Then in the sixth century in Italy St Benedict emerged and wrote a *Rule* for his monks at Montecassino in a time of great confusion in the West. In time it became the dominant rule for monks in the West and the monks who followed it came to be called Benedictines. It was the *Rule* which united them. They were not an order but each abbey was an independent community or family.

There were many changes and developments through the Middle Ages and the monasteries suffered greatly by being absorbed into and adopted by feudalism. But the monastic ideal survived. It survived also the upheaval of the Reformation and began to find new expressions of an ancient ideal. There was a revival of the English Benedictines and they survived on the Continent until the French Revolution, after which they found refuge again in England. In the nineteenth century, the English Priory of St Laurence struck down new roots at Ampleforth in North Yorkshire.

Influences on the Young Basil Hume

William Charles

During his early years in the monastery, the young Brother Basil was subject to a number of influences. While it is not the aim of this piece to provide an exhaustive guide to the studies of a young monk in the 1940s, perhaps it may be useful to give some indication of the ideas that shaped his mind.

It was of course the case that appropriate time would have been spent learning about monasticism, the *Rule of St Benedict*, the scriptures, and many other aspects of religious life. The monks were also encouraged to learn about the spiritual life through the writings of a variety of spiritual writers. For the novices of the time, one very influential writer was the Benedictine Abbot Columba Marmion.

Abbot Marmion was renowned as a retreat-giver and writer. His writings repay study. Pope John Paul II reportedly said, 'I owe more to Columba Marmion for initiating me into things spiritual than to any other spiritual writer.' His most popular book, *Christ the Life of the Soul*, is a classic. In it, Marmion points out that God's essential quality is holiness. He sets great store by the teaching that

God has adopted all humanity as his children and that we therefore have the right to approach him as a child approaches a loving father. As the title implies, Marmion is concerned that his readers understand the implications of baptism. For Christian churches teach that Christ enters into a soul at the moment of baptism and remains there always. It is part of Christians' responsibility to nurture the life of Christ in their souls and to look for him in others, given that, as the Book of Genesis teaches, each of us is made in the image and likeness of God. Basil later advised 'see him in the gardener ... in your friends ... in everyone'.

It is impossible to say just how much Basil absorbed the influence of Abbot Marmion from reading his books. Much he will have got indirectly from monks like Father Placid Dolan and Father Stephen Marwood, who were immersed in Marmion. Whichever way, the idea of Christ in the soul and the warmer spirituality associated with it became an important influence and helped him, over time, to a much friendlier idea of God than he had received as a child.

Ampleforth had a hall of residence at Oxford. It was here therefore that Basil went in 1944 to take a degree in history.

The education provided was important for Basil. Oxford teaching, based on the tutorial system, challenges students in a special way. The student is required to prepare his ideas before a tutorial and discuss them with an expert in the subject. As a teaching method, it requires the student to prepare very thoroughly, to have read a considerable amount in the time available and to have thought carefully about the subject being discussed. It can be an enormously powerful teaching approach, instilling into the students habits of careful preparation and openness of mind, a willingness to recognize that one's first ideas may have been wrong and that there may be relevant ideas which have simply not crossed the student's minds at all. It can teach students very effectively the limits of their competence.

Certainly, Basil in later life showed not only much humility but also considerable openness of mind. For example, in his book *Towards a Civilization of Love*, he considered the possibility that there may be other forms of intelligent life elsewhere in the universe.

A far more important influence for Basil, though, was his next course at Fribourg in Switzerland, where he went in 1947 to study theology with the Dominicans. It was here for the first time that he seriously encountered the works of the thirteenth-century friar St Thomas Aquinas.

St Thomas is generally regarded as one of the greatest theologians. For many who take an interest in his work it may be that he is remembered above all for applying methods learned from Aristotle, the classical Greek philosopher and master of logic, to the study of Christian theology. His achievement in reconciling the two is widely considered a major intellectual triumph. However, Aquinas's principal significance for Basil is to be found elsewhere.

St Thomas has a vision of the universe which is profoundly satisfying. For he teaches that all creation flows from God in a single and continuing expression of God's overwhelming goodness and love. God, being love and a creator, makes a universe in which all creation in some way reflects the nature of the creative artist. Thus all that is beautiful, good or true in some way reflects the nature of the underlying Creator. All humans are made in some degree in the image of God, and are, whether they know it or not, in search of their maker, who is also in search of them. So, all creation is a continuing outpouring from God, who is at the same time calling creation back. The reader who remembers the young Basil's love of Wordsworth will see how Aquinas's teaching will have resonated with his feeling that God reveals himself in creation.

St Thomas also addressed Basil's youthful ponderings on the subject of happiness. For he said:

> I eventually found a master to teach and guide me ... St
> Thomas reflected on the subject of happiness. He argued
> that we were indeed made for happiness, for beatitude. But
> the kind of happiness for which we crave must have two
> qualities if it is to be totally satisfying. First it must be
> complete, leaving us with no other desires, and secondly it
> must be permanent.
>
> Cardinal Basil Hume, *The Mystery of the Incarnation*
> (Darton Longman and Todd 1999)

So, complete happiness could only be found in a complete
and permanent being, that is in God.

St Thomas's vision provided Basil with a view of the
universe that made sense. It enriched his prayer life and its
influence can be seen frequently in his teachings and
writings in later life. He would so often refer to the beautiful,
the good and the true as providing glimpses of the reality of
God.

Brother Brendan, a contemporary of his at Ampleforth,
who also went to Fribourg, remembered Basil excitedly
coming into his room to talk about their course, drawing
diagrams to illustrate the ideas which studying Aquinas's
theology had given him. Brother Brendan believed that this
was the time when Basil 'came alive' intellectually.

Basil found other important treasures in St Thomas's
work. One was his emphasis on teaching with argument and
discussion, not by reliance on authority. Another significant
discovery was St Thomas's teaching on morality, for it
contrasted with the teaching that had been fashionable
while Basil was growing up and which concentrated on
behaviour which was forbidden. Aquinas's teaching was
concerned far more with teaching what it meant to be a
good person: what was virtue and how should humans seek
to be good? Aquinas has a fundamentally positive view of
humanity and Basil found this appealing and in later years
would compare him with St Augustine, a writer with a

sometimes less positive outlook. Usually Basil would opt for Aquinas's view.

I benefited from his teaching on morality when young, for he would talk to me regularly, emphasizing that happiness was to be found in serving others in accordance with God's will, in giving rather than receiving.

St Thomas remained for the rest of Basil's life the single most important influence on his thinking. Basil acknowledged his debt to St Thomas often in later years, even quoting on occasions a Dominican motto: '*contemplata aliis tradere*' – to pass on to others things which have been contemplated. It could have been a motto for his own life.

Basil also learned from St Thomas's teaching about life after death. Aquinas teaches that heaven will be friendship with God and that, if we get there, we will enjoy a vision of God, known as the Beatific Vision. Basil described it as: 'that ecstasy of love which the vision of God is going to be.' Basil would often say: 'We are made for that.'

The fact that Aquinas had so much influence on Basil doubtless results from a number of factors. The Benedictines, as the one religious order who came through the most difficult part of the Dark Ages in Europe, provided the base for religious life as matters improved in the first centuries of the second millennium. The Dominicans learned much from them. Indeed, Aquinas started his religious life with the Benedictines. He laid great emphasis on truth; Basil was a very truthful person. Aquinas stressed the need to keep searching; Basil saw his whole life as a search for God. Aquinas turned to prayer when uncertain of the way forward, an approach which will have resonated deeply with Basil. Finally, Aquinas advised people to heal their desires, not suppress them. Basil, with his kind acceptance of people and following the Benedictine tradition, shared this attitude.